BEC
Higher Testbuilder

Anthea Bazin and Elaine Boyd

D1697725

MACMILLAN

Macmillan Education
Between Towns Road, Oxford OX4 3PP
A division of Macmillan Publishers Limited
Companies and representatives throughout the world

ISBN: 978-0-230-71701-5

Text © Anthea Bazin and Elaine Boyd 2009
Design and illustration © Macmillan Publishers Limited 2009

First published 2009

Designed by xen
Cover design by Macmillan
Recorded by James Richardson at The Soundhouse Studios

Authors' acknowledgements
The authors would like to thank Sarah Dymond for her expert
advice and useful suggestions on the exam tasks and strategies
and Xanthe Sturt Taylor for her superb editorial assistance.

The authors and publisher are grateful for permission to reprint
the following copyright material:
Test 1 Reading Part 1 – Article 'Management Consultancy: unleash
your big ideas' by Kate Hilpern, copyright © The Independent
2007, first published in The Independent 18.10.07, reprinted by
permission of the publisher.
Test 1 Reading Part 2 – Article 'Is it change, or the past preserved?'
by Dr James Rieley, copyright © The Telegraph Group Limited
2005, first published in The Telegraph 28.01.05, reprinted by
permission of the publisher.
Test 1 Reading Part 3 – Article 'Big Brands turning to Big Brother'
by Stephen Hoare, copyright © The Telegraph Group Limited,
reprinted by permission of the publisher.
Test 1 Reading Part 4 – Article 'From Buckingham Palace to the
dairy farms of Argentina…' by Stephen Pritchard, copyright © The
Independent 2008, first published in The Independent 10.02.08,
reprinted by permission of the publisher.
Test 1 Reading Part 5 – Article ' Murphy's Law waits to catch out
the unwary' by Michael Becket, copyright © The Telegraph Group
Limited 2003, first published in The Telegraph 07.05.03, reprinted
by permission of the publisher.
Test 1 Reading Part 6 – Article 'Evans cycles to a more Active
future' by Yvette Essen, copyright © Telegraph Group Limited
2008, first published in The Telegraph 06.04.08, reprinted by
permission of the publisher.
Test 2 Reading Part 1 – Article 'Building a Tribe' by Mike Southon,
copyright © Telegraph Group Limited 2007, first published in The
Telegraph 04.09.07, reprinted by permission of the publisher.
Test 2 Reading Part 2 – Article 'My Best Deal' by Andrew Cave,
copyright © Telegraph Group Limited 2007, first published in The
Telegraph 27.04.07, reprinted by permission of the publisher.
Test 2 Reading Part 3 – Article 'How mags get goods into bags' by
James Hall, copyright © Telegraph Group Limited, first published
in The Telegraph, reprinted by permission of the publisher.
Test 2 Reading Part 4 – Article 'Don't quit your job until you're
ready' by Professor Russell Smith, copyright © The Independent,
first published in The Independent, reprinted by permission of the
publisher.
Test 2 Reading Part 5 – Article ' Working from home carries a cost'
by Emma Lunn, copyright © Telegraph Group Limited 2006, first
published in The Telegraph 31.03.06, reprinted by permission of
the publisher.

Test 2 Reading Part 6 – Article ' Get your message to the media' by
Robert Leaf, copyright © Robert Leaf 2007, first published in The
Telegraph 24.08.07, reprinted by permission of the author
Test 3 Reading 1 – Article 'Secrets behind a business marriage
made in heaven' by Brian Bloch, copyright © Telegraph Group
Limited 2007, first published in The Telegraph 12.10.07, reprinted
by permission of the publisher.
Test 3 Reading 2 – Article ' The truth about work: It's a no brainer
to save real training for managers' by David Bolchover, copyright
© Telegraph Group Limited 2006, first published in The Telegraph
06.03.06, reprinted by permission of the publisher.
Test 3 Reading 3 – Article 'A Little Anarchy at work can do a world
of good' by Brian Bloch, copyright © Telegraph Group Limited,
first published in The Telegraph, reprinted by permission of the
publisher.
Test 3 Reading 4 – Article 'Asda creating 3,900 jobs in expansion
drive', copyright © Telegraph Group Limited 2003, first published
in The Telegraph 18.02.03, reprinted by permission of the
publisher.
Test 4 Reading 1 – Article 'The Big Question: Why is John Lewis
giving staff a 20% bonus and why is it doing so well' by Michael
Savage, copyright © The Independent 2008, first published in The
Independent 07.03.08, reprinted by permission of the publisher.
Test 4 Reading 2 – Article 'How a management technique designed
for factories has taken root outdoors' by Robert Miller, copyright
© Telegraph Group Limited 2005, first published in The Telegraph
21.07.05, reprinted by permission of the publisher.
Test 4 Reading 3 – Article 'Selling should be easy' by Mike
Southon, copyright © Telegraph Group Limited 2007, first
published in The Telegraph 26.10.07, reprinted by permission of
the publisher.
Test 4 Reading 4 – Article ' It's often those on the shop floor who
can spot the best business ideas' by Roger Trapp, copyright © The
Independent 2008, first published in The Independent 04.03.08,
reprinted by permission of the publisher.
Test 4 Reading 5 – Article 'Sorry I can't take your call right
now. I'm in a meeting…' by Chris Goodall, copyright © The
Independent 2007, first published in The Independent 12.08.07,
reprinted by permission of the publisher.
Test 4 Reading 6 – Article 'Construction 1' by Liza Smith, copyright
© Liza Smith , first published in The Independent 01.02.08.

Reading and Listening Answer Sheets – Reproduced with the
permission of Cambridge ESOL.

Printed and bound in Thailand

2013 2012 2011 2010 2009
10 9 8 7 6 5 4 3 2 1

CONTENTS

BEC Higher Testbuilder

The BEC Higher Testbuilder provides students with the information and practice they need to pass BEC Higher. It offers teachers and students an encouraging and accessible way to prepare for the exam and may be used as part of a business English course or as a self-access programme for students preparing for the exam on their own. There are four complete practice tests that reflect the content and level of the actual examination. All the tests are of a similar standard and include the themes, topics and vocabulary specified in the BEC Higher Syllabus. They are accompanied by an expanded answer key and further practice and guidance pages.

Key and Explanation

The main purpose of the key and explanation is to promote confidence and understanding of the demands of the exam. It gives students and teachers information about why a particular answer is correct and, when appropriate, there are explanations as to why other options or possible answers are incorrect.

Further Practice and Guidance pages

Each part of the test is accompanied by one or more further practice and guidance pages. The aim of these pages is to give students more information about how to tackle the particular item types in that part of the test and to help them develop the independence and confidence to check their own answers to the test questions. There are also graduated exercises to enable them to improve their test technique as well as their language skills.

How to use the BEC Higher Testbuilder

1   Follow the instructions given at the end of each part of the test.

    If there are Further Practice pages relating to that part you can:

a   complete one part of a paper, perhaps under exam conditions, and then either do the Further Practice pages relating to that part, check the answers to the Further Practice questions and then review the test questions, taking into consideration what you have practised. Then you check the answers to the test questions and go through the explanations.

OR

b   check the answers to the test questions you have just done and go through the explanations if there are no Further Practice activities.

2   Vary the order. You may wish to do some of the Further Practice and Guidance pages before answering the part of the test they relate to.

Note to teachers

As an alternative to the above, you may wish to do the Further Practice and Guidance pages as discussion or pairwork, or ask students to prepare them before class.

Business English Certificate (Higher level)

The BEC examination covers the four language skills of reading, writing, listening and speaking.

Reading (1 hour)

The Reading Test is in six parts. There are 52 questions, worth one mark each.

Part One

This is a matching task based on five short texts or one longer text divided into five sections (approximately 450 words in total). The texts are taken from newspapers, magazines, catalogues and company reports. The task is to match eight statements to the relevant text. This part of the text focuses on your ability to identify gist and global meaning. See pages 10 and 96 for Further Practice and Guidance.

Part Two

This is a matching task consisting of a single text (450–500 words in total) such as an article or a report that has had seven sentences removed from it, and a set of eight sentences. There is one sentence which you do not need to use. The task is to choose one of the set of eight sentences to fit into each gap. The first one is done as an example so you only have to complete six gaps. This part tests your understanding of text structure as well as general comprehension of the text as a whole. See pages 40 and 96 for Further Practice and Guidance.

Part Three

This task is a single text (500–600 words) with six four-option multiple choice questions. The text may be a newspaper article or some business literature including company information and management topics. This part tests your ability to understand the text as a whole as well as specific details. It also tests opinion and inference. See pages 70 and 96 for Further Practice and Guidance.

Part Four

This is a single text (approximately 250 words) with eleven gaps. The first one is done as an example. The task is to select the correct answer from a choice of four options. This part tests your vocabulary and understanding of structure. See pages 18 and 102 for Further Practice and Guidance.

Part Five

This is a single text (approximately 250 words) with eleven gaps. The first one is done for you as an example. The task is to decide which word fits correctly in the gap. You are not given the words but have to decide for yourself. This part tests your understanding of structure and discourse features. See pages 47 and 102 for Further Practice and Guidance.

Part Six

This is a proof reading task. The task is to identify words that have been introduced incorrectly into the text. The text (150–200 words) could be a letter, an advertisement, a short article or other similar material. See pages 76 and 102 for Further Practice and Guidance.

Writing (1 hour 10 minutes)

The Writing Test is in two parts. There are a total of ten possible marks for the first part and a total of twenty possible marks for the second part.

Part One

This task is to produce a report (120–140 words) using the information given in some graphic input. The instructions explain what the graphic input shows and tells you how to summarise the information, e.g. comparing, etc. The input may consist of graphs, bar charts or pie charts of the type frequently used in the business pages of newspapers or company reports or brochures. This part tests your ability to describe and compare figures and make inferences from the information given. See page 23 for Further Practice and Guidance.

Part Two

This task is to produce a longer piece of writing (200–250 words) using your own experience and knowledge of the world of work to guide the content. You are given a choice of three tasks: a report, a piece of business correspondence, e.g. a letter, and a proposal. In each case you are given instructions which give you a reason for writing and tell you who you are writing to. This part tests your ability to describe, summarise, reassure, explain, apologise, complain, recommend or persuade. See pages 51, 79 and 105 for Further Practice and Guidance.

Listening (40 minutes)

The Listening Test consists of recorded extracts and a written question paper. In the exam, the instructions are on the recording and on the question paper. The test is in three parts and lasts about 30 minutes. In the exam, each section is heard twice and there is an extra ten minutes to transfer the answers on to a special answer sheet. There are 30 questions worth one mark each.

Part One

This part is a monologue, usually by someone giving a speech or a presentation. The task is to complete the gaps in twelve sentences or notes with a word or words (maximum 3) from the monologue. This part tests your ability to listen for factual or specific information. Correct spelling of the word or words in the answer is expected. See pages 27 and 111 for Further Practice and Guidance.

Part Two

This part has two sections that have to be completed as one task. You will hear five short monologues from five different speakers. The task is to match each monologue to one option in each set of eight options. There is a theme or topic linking the two sets of options. This part tests your global listening skills and your ability to understand the main idea or gist of the monologues. See pages 55 and 111 for Further Practice and Guidance.

Part Three

There is a longer text in this part of 4–5 minutes. This is an interview, discussion or conversation. There are eight three-option multiple choice questions that test your general understanding of ideas and opinions expressed in the recording. See pages 85 and 111 for Further Practice and Guidance.

Speaking (16 minutes)

The Speaking Test is taken either in pairs or, occasionally, with three candidates. There are two examiners. One of them (the interlocutor) will speak to you and lead you through the tasks. The other examiner just listens. Both examiners are involved in the marking process. The test is in three parts.

Part One

This part lasts about three minutes. The interlocutor will speak to each of you in turn and ask you general questions about your life, your work or your studies. You are being tested on your ability to talk briefly about yourself and to show you are able to agree, disagree or express preferences. You won't usually be asked exactly the same questions as your partner. See pages 33 and 116 for Further Practice and Guidance.

Part Two

In this part of the test, you will be asked to give a mini-presentation on a business topic. You and your partner are each given a choice of three topics and you have one minute to prepare your presentation. You are expected to talk for about one minute. When you have finished your presentation, your partner is invited to ask you one or two questions about it. This part tests your ability to speak for an extended period. See pages 61 and 116 for Further Practice and Guidance.

Part Three

In Part Three, you and your partner are given a topic to discuss for about four minutes. The topic is given on a prompt card followed by two (or three for three candidates) discussion points. You are expected to reach some decisions, but it is acceptable for you to disagree with each other as long as this is expressed clearly. The interlocutor will then ask questions related to the topic. This part tests your ability to hold a conversation, express opinions, compare and contrast and agree or disagree. See pages 89 and 116 for Further Practice and Guidance.

BEC TEST 1

Reading

PART ONE

Questions 1–8

- Look at the statements below and at the five extracts from an article on the opposite page about working in the field of management consultancy.

- Which extract (**A, B, C, D** or **E**) does each statement (**1–8**) refer to?

- For each statement **1–8**, mark one letter (**A, B, C, D** or **E**) on your Answer Sheet.

- You will need to use some of these letters more than once.

- There is an example at the beginning, (**0**).

Example:

    0   Consultants may be able to work for a specialist firm.

0	A	B	C	D	E
	☐	▓	☐	☐	☐

---

1   Consultants must be prepared to change the way they have evaluated a project.

2   Consultants need to value the colleagues they work with.

3   Large consultancies often have a background in accounting.

4   Consultants need to be able to assess each person's contribution accurately.

5   You can become a consultant even if you have no management experience.

6   Mentoring is often used to help trainees become more effective at the job.

7   Consultancy work is satisfying because you see the end result of a project.

8   Consultants must not be frightened of being honest.

Before you check your answers to Part One, go on to pages 10–11.

A 5 6

A good proportion of people entering consultancy do so after several years of industry experience. Those who have gone through a big graduate programme, have climbed the career ladder quickly and who have an MBA behind them tend to be favoured. But fear not – if you are a team player with sharp intellect, ambition and good communication skills, consultancy firms may be willing to train you up themselves. New entrants will usually join an intensive induction and training period under the guidance of an experienced consultant. During that time, you'll develop your skills and experience and gain ever more responsibility for the detailed day-to-day conduct of an assignment.

B 3

Employers, like consultancy work itself, are very varied. You could opt for a generalist consulting firm, which offers a wide range of services from strategy consulting and human resources to IT and, in some cases, outsourcing on a global basis. Many of these firms grew out of audit firms, while others developed within IT service companies. Alternatively, you could join a strategy consultancy. These tend to be much smaller than the generalist firms and the majority are American. As the term suggests, they primarily offer strategic advice to companies on a project-by-project basis.

C 7

Fiona Czerniawska, director of the Management Consultancies Association Think Tank, believes there's never been a better time to become a management consultant. "When you describe what's involved in management consultancy – going to meetings, gathering data and writing reports – it doesn't exactly sound exciting," admits Czerniawska. "But in fact, consultants get to spend a lot of time really listening to clients, helping them to articulate the issue they are grappling with and resolving the problem. If you take the analogy of a doctor, it's like being able to both diagnose a health problem and do the surgery."

D 1 4 2

Cathy Monghan, head of the HR consultancy PES, adds that consultants need resilience: "You need to be able to prioritise and then inevitably reprioritise in accordance with the client's needs," she says. Meanwhile, Peter Walker, executive chairman of Pielle Consulting Group, believes consultants should also be "capable of seeing a whole picture from fragments of information, able to determine the key to moving to the next step and have a very clear appreciation of the law of unforeseen consequences." He adds, "They also need to be a team player with the ambition to be captain and the humility to recognise the importance of every member of the team."

E 8 4

Olwyn Burgess, client services director of HR consultancy Chiumento, agrees that sophisticated team skills are key. "Consultants have to be astute enough to spot the people who can help and those that will hinder the progress of a project and then have a strategy to work with or around the enablers and blockers," he adds. "You have to tell it how it is," adds Tom Barry, BlessingWhite European managing director. "For example, there will be occasions when you have to advise a client on something you know won't be popular. This is all part and parcel of providing consultancy. You need that strong spine."

Further practice for Reading Part One

EXAM INFORMATION

Part One of the Reading Test is a matching task and consists of five short texts on a related theme (or sometimes a single text divided into five sections). The texts may include:

- advertisements for goods or services
- extracts from company reports
- job advertisements
- book reviews
- business or career advice
- business news articles

You are given eight statements and you have to say to which of the five texts each statement refers.

A DETAILED STUDY

In this part of the test you need to be able to carefully analyse the statements in order to check which text contains ALL the information in the statement. Similar information or wording may occur in more than one text but only one will match the statement. In order to identify the correct text, you need to be able to identify key information and not get distracted by any extra or irrelevant information.

For example, five texts may all contain advice on recruiting staff. Look at these extracts:

A

You should use an agency if you're struggling to find staff that are specific to your sector as they have more experience at this and some specialise, for example, in production or clerical staff.

B

Many managers don't have the time to see all potential recruits themselves so hand over the initial processes to the support staff in your office. It is only managers who expect to be interviewed by equals.

C

It is a good idea to source a firm of headhunters for any more senior roles. Looking for the ideal person who is already in your field can eat up an enormous amount of your resources, not least of which is time, plus you may not have the necessary contacts.

D

If you are looking for people who are experienced then your job ad should always clearly state exactly what experience you require. This is especially true in more senior roles and will save you time in the long run as it will weed out people who are unsuitable.

E

Often when you are recruiting managerial roles, the person you need may not have enough spare time to attend an interview, especially if they are in another location. In this case, do an interview over the phone initially to check if they have the type of experience you require and to allow them to ask questions.

The statement which has to be matched is:

Ask for external help if you are looking for someone who [1]has worked in your sector [2]in a high level role but [3]you are too busy to deal with the recruitment.

The statement refers to the piece of advice that is for people who need to recruit:

1 experienced staff
2 for a managerial job
3 but don't have the time

So you can see that only extract C contains all three elements in this statement.

1   Read the extracts about being a management consultant on page 9, and then answer these questions. Which extract is most appropriate if

    1   you're concerned consultancy work may be unsatisfying?

    2   you want to know how confident you need to be?

    3   you want to know what kind of background you need?

    4   you want to know what types of consultancy work are offered?

    5   you want to know how flexible you need to be?

2   Look at the five extracts on page 9 again. Underline all the references to:

    1   outcomes

    2   attitudes and/or behaviour

    3   skills

3   You will need to decide key words in the statements, then identify this information in the texts. Now underline the key words in each of the statements on page 8.

4   The extracts will contain paraphrases of the key words in the statements. Look at the statements again on page 8 and write paraphrases for these words. Use words from the extracts and any others you may know.

    0   specialist   *an expert in*

    1   change

    2   value

    3   accounting

    4   assess

    5   no

    6   mentoring

    7   end result

    8   being honest

Now check your answers to these questions and look back at your answers to Part One of the Reading Test.

PART TWO

Questions 9–14

* Read this text taken from an article about helping the people who manage change.
* Choose the best sentence from the opposite page to fill each of the gaps.
* For each gap **9–14**, mark one letter (**A–H**) on your Answer Sheet.
* Do not use any letter more than once.
* There is an example at the beginning, (**0**).

Is it change, or the past preserved?

Last week, I received a letter from a reader who was concerned that the people who were leading the change effort in his company were not competent to do so. He asked: "How can I show them what they really need to do if they don't see it themselves?" **(0)** ...H.... . About the only way to ensure people decide to do something differently is to help them see the gap between what they do now and what they need to do in the future. **(9)** ..D... . This means that, if you can help them see the gaps between where they want to go (and why), and where they are now and what skills they need to drive change, the potential for improvement is increased.

To identify the gap, assemble a small group of managers and discuss what the goal is and why. **(10)** ..B... . The numbers are just the end result. What you want to be able to see are the dimensions of the organisation that will drive those results. You should do this with more than one group. **(11)** ..G... . What you have to consider is all aspects of the organisation. Try questions such as, "What systems and processes will be needed in the future?" Or, "What reward structures will be needed?" Or even, "What competencies will be needed?" When you get some consensus, compare it with what is in place at the moment. **(12)** ..A... . But because your competition is closing their gaps, you have to as well.

Next, sit down with the managers who have to implement the change programme and show them the consensus on what has to be achieved. **(13)** ..F.... . If you want this effort to succeed, ask them what they will do differently in four managerial competency areas: how they think, how they influence, how they achieve and how they lead.

After they have done this, they need to do a peer and subordinate review. Historically, when doing this review, managers discover that what they have done in the past will not cut it in the future. Yes, you may experience rejection or looks of bewilderment. **(14)** ..C.. . If the organisation is to change for the better, managers need to realise that the only way it will happen is if they do things differently. And the only effective way for them to do this is to see it themselves.

Example:

A Rest assured, there will be a gap and, in some organisations, the gap is rather intimidating.

B This is important; they need to look at more than just the financial aspects.

C But managers need to realise that the organisation is the way it is because of past decisions and the way they acted on them.

D All the talking in the world about changing the way people work will not carry any weight compared with managers and employees discovering the gap themselves.

E This is lame, old thinking that is not sustainable nor workable.

F Then ask them what they are prepared to do differently, beginning tomorrow, to close the gaps.

G Different managers have different perspectives and it is always good to see if there is a consensus in how the challenge is seen.

H My experience is that you can't.

PART THREE

Questions 15–20

- Read the following extract from an article about a specialised form of market research, and the questions on the opposite page.

- For each question **15–20**, mark one letter (**A, B, C** or **D**) on your Answer Sheet for the answer you choose.

Big brands turning to Big Brother

Questionnaires and focus groups aren't enough – now companies are having volunteers filmed for days on end to see what makes customers
5 *really tick.*

Innovation is the norm in our fickle, fast-moving consumer culture. But launching new products or repositioning faded
10 brands is increasingly the subject of scientific scrutiny. As development costs escalate so do the risks of a commercial failure. Global brands want to make sure
15 their products succeed across national boundaries and are turning for help to a new kind of market testing – ethnographic research.

20 In less than a decade ethnographic research – detailed observations of the day-to-day behaviours of a small sample from a target group of consumers
25 to shed light on how they use, choose or buy products – has established itself alongside consumer surveys and focus groups as a leading tool of market
30 research.

Siamack Salari, boss of one firm specialising in this field called EverydayLives, explains ethnographic research as social
35 anthropology meets the internet. Salari's researchers follow paid volunteers for days filming their every move with a hand-held camcorder in order to uncover
40 hidden truths about the way they lead their lives. Some time, usually towards the end of the first day, the novelty of

being filmed will wear off and
45 unselfconscious behaviours will start to emerge. The best insights come when people are feeling relaxed and off their guard. Hours and hours of video are
50 analysed for key behaviours before being finally edited down to around an hour of film that can be played back to the subject and shared with the client.

55 To research any given product, a sample is constructed usually of no more than six individuals or households each of which is filmed for two to three days.
60 Then, as Salari explains, the hard work begins – analysing and interpreting behaviours. Film has the advantage over questionnaires because the
65 camera doesn't lie. People are often unaware of how they appear feeding the cat, for example, or chatting with other family members, or shopping in a
70 supermarket aisle. Salari explains: "What the subject didn't do or nearly did can often reveal far more about their inner motives than what is happening on the
75 surface."

The discussion between researcher and subject is used to generate insights which Salari calls 'co-discoveries'.
80 Describing his own brand of ethnography as "observational research with common sense and lateral thinking thrown in", Salari points out that only
85 this type of qualitative research offers unexpected insights. While supermarkets mine data

from micro-chipped loyalty cards to segment markets and
90 target special offers, this kind of number-crunching misses the bigger picture of how products are chosen and how they could be improved.

95 Salari points out: "Ethnographic research is always agenda-less. It's totally opposed to other forms of research and its big benefit is that it generates insights." Sometimes
100 ethnographic research suggests small changes that can make the difference between a product succeeding in its market or falling flat. Such insight does not come
105 cheap, however. According to Salari, an observational survey would cost in the region of £4,000–£6,000 per household. Normally a minimum of six households
110 would participate.

Ethnographic research is widely endorsed and has gained in popularity through word of mouth. London Business School
115 even devotes its latest MBA core module – discovering entrepreneurial opportunities – to expounding the principles of ethnographic research, and
120 MBA students borrow heavily on these skills in their business start-up competition. John Mullins, assistant professor of entrepreneurship at LBS, says:
125 "We use only ethnographic and qualitative research – in-depth observation – because a long list of the best and biggest companies are doing it to discover real
130 customer insights and to satisfy their needs."

15 What does the writer say about new products in the first paragraph?

    A Detailed research will ensure that new products are successful.

    B New products have to be available worldwide nowadays.

    C Companies are more reluctant to take risks than previously.

    D Consumers will stop buying brands that fail to innovate.

16 In the second paragraph we learn that the advantage of ethnographic research is that

    A other people can watch participants' behaviour.

    B people are unaware that they are being filmed.

    C it is easy to gather large amounts of data.

    D it can capture previously unknown information.

17 What does Solari say is the advantage of using a camera?

    A It allows for more accurate data to be collected.

    B Participants don't need to complete any paperwork.

    C Several people can be filmed at the same time.

    D Data can be collected over a short period.

18 In the fifth paragraph, Solari says the disadvantage of supermarket loyalty cards is that

    A the data they deliver is predictable.

    B they are only useful for certain specific purposes.

    C they don't allow for human interpretation of data.

    D they need to be improved to deliver more information.

19 In the sixth paragraph, how does Solari say ethnographic research can improve products?

    A Although expensive to begin with, it can reduce costs in the long term.

    B It offers objective information on how a product will perform.

    C It selects a small range of participants that are likely to buy the product.

    D It can highlight a key issue before the product is launched.

20 How does ethnographic research fit into the programmes at the London Business School?

    A It is the only form of research it approves for its students.

    B It is promoted as a research method on one of its courses.

    C MBA students must use this method in a business competition.

    D Large companies advise the School on how to use this form of research.

PART FOUR

Questions 21–30

- Read the article below about smartphones.
- Choose the correct word to fill each gap from **A, B, C** or **D** on the opposite page.
- For each question **21–30**, mark one letter (**A, B, C** or **D**) on your Answer Sheet.
- There is an example at the beginning, (**0**).

Smartphones – a necessity or a luxury?

Smartphones have (**0**) ..D.. beyond the boardroom and keeping a close eye on what's new is Mike Lazaridis, chief executive of RIM, the company that makes the BlackBerry smartphone. His device may no longer be quite as trendy as it once was but it is still (**21**) ..... – particularly for Argentinian milk farmers. Mr Lazaridis says: "I like the way it's being used by the farmers so they are always up to date. Milk is a (**22**) ..... item, so delivery and production standards are incredibly important." He is reminded of the company's early days: "This is where we started in 1987, with a wireless vertical data business for the Swedish lumber (**23**) ....., and then on to fire brigades, ambulances and garbage trucks."

While the BlackBerry was quick to (**24**) ..... itself as the accessory of choice for business professionals such as Wall Street traders, the cheaper price (**25**) ..... and new, more colourful handsets now (**26**) ..... offer have opened it up to a much wider market. Mr Lazaridis says: "It was obvious that business people and self-employed professionals would buy the BlackBerry, but we were not expecting the (**27**) ..... we had from ordinary consumers."

The greatest challenge for RIM, however, could lie in an economic (**28**) ....., when individuals and companies alike may see devices like the BlackBerry as luxuries they can (**29**) ..... without. The company has to make its product indispensable to the lifestyles of consumers, or prove that they bring a real (**30**) ..... on investment for business users.

Example:

A unfolded   B widened   C displayed   D spread

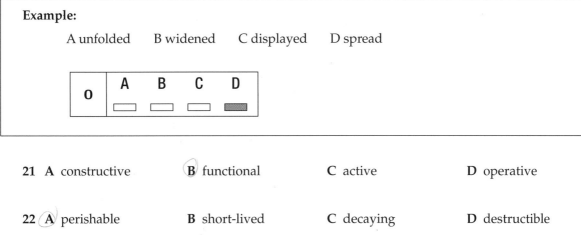

O	A	B	C	D
	☐	☐	☐	▓

21 **A** constructive   **B** functional   **C** active   **D** operative

22 **A** perishable   **B** short-lived   **C** decaying   **D** destructible

23 **A** manufacturers   **B** enterprise   **C** commerce   **D** industry

24 **A** install   **B** establish   **C** create   **D** demonstrate

25 **A** designs   **B** programmes   **C** plans   **D** systems

26 **A** at   **B** on   **C** for   **D** under

27 **A** return   **B** retort   **C** reply   **D** response

28 **A** downturn   **B** fall   **C** decrease   **D** drop

29 **A** make   **B** carry   **C** do   **D** stay

30 **A** return   **B** gain   **C** interest   **D** profit

Before you check your answers to Part Four, go on to pages 18–19.

Further practice for Reading Part Four

EXAM INFORMATION

Part Four consists of a text with eleven gaps. The first one is done for you as an example. You have to choose the word that best fits each gap from ten four-option multiple choice items. Most of the items test vocabulary. The options are all from the same part of speech but only one option fits the meaning. This part of the test is designed to see if you can distinguish between words of similar meaning.

A DETAILED STUDY

1   *You should always read the text first to get a general sense of meaning. Answer the following questions to help you with the general meaning of the text.*

    1   Why is the Blackberry still used by some farmers?

    2   Where did the company start?

    3   Who was the Blackberry popular with originally?

    4   What has happened to the Blackberry now?

    5   What may threaten the popularity of the Blackberry?

    6   What must the company do to retain its popularity?

2   *To improve and widen your vocabulary, you will need to check dictionary definitions. Match each of the following words to their definitions. All the words are options in the test.*

    1   **A** constructive   **B** functional   **C** active   **D** operative

        1   useful; working correctly

        2   working and able to be used

        3   suggestions or input that is intended to improve something

        4   still in good working order

    2   **A** perishable   **B** short-lived   **C** decaying   **D** destructible

        1   starting to rot or becoming destroyed

        2   existing or happening for only a limited time

        3   can be damaged so that it can no longer be used

        4   likely to decay quickly

    3   **A** response   **B** return   **C** retort   **D** reply

        1   a written or spoken answer to an enquiry

        2   to act or speak after something has happened or been said

        3   an angry or humorous remark

        4   a statement giving a written answer to official questions

    4   **A** install   **B** establish   **C** create   **D** demonstrate

        1   to show or describe how something works

        2   to put a piece of equipment somewhere and connect it so it can be used

        3   to start an organization or system that is intended to continue for some time

        4   to make something exist that did not exist before

3 *In order to select the right word you will have to look carefully at the words before and after the gap to see which option fits best. Certain words typically collocate with certain other words, e.g. According to ... .*

For each of the following, match the word that each option often collocates with. All the words are options from the test.

1

A	to do something by	**1**	plan
B	under a	**2**	design
C	a change of	**3**	system
D	to come to the end of a	**4**	programme

2

A	at	**1**	sale
B	on	**2**	cost
C	for	**3**	control
D	under	**4**	offer

3

A	a return	**1**	of
B	a gain	**2**	in
C	an interest	**3**	on
D	a profit	**4**	of

Now check your answers to these questions and look back at your answers to Part Four of the Reading Test.

PART FIVE

Questions 31–40

- Read the article below about booking conference venues.
- For each question **31–40**, write one word in CAPITAL LETTERS on your Answer Sheet.
- There is an example at the beginning, (**0**).

Example: | **0** | N | O | T | | | | |

How to book a conference

First decision is the choice of venue. Which venue is right will depend (**0**) .....
just on the number of people attending. It will also depend on the cost (**31**) and
whether the participants (**32**) are being charged to attend. If the event lasts
for several days the problem of finding accommodation influences the choice,
but just (**33**) to complicate the decision it also depends on whether to have
everybody on the same premises as the conference. Some seminars break up
the sessions   (**34**) from time to time into smaller groups which will require
additional rooms with the right facilities. (**35**) They really do need to be handy
for the main session.

Professionals advise not (**36**) to book any premises or facilities without
visiting first. In (**37**) any case, you need to meet the senior organising staff to
find out what they can do and what they have. And it is probably a good idea
to test all the equipment and ask about back-ups.

A frustrating problem for organisers laying on the facilities is never being sure
just (**38**) how many people will turn up. People go sick, managers (**39**) who were
overseas suddenly reappear, an emergency at the company prevents some key
people attending, and (**40**) so on. Still, some estimate is vital for the booking.
It may be indeed one of the factors in deciding the venue and in haggling over
the price. If all that sounds just too much hassle there is another option – hire a
professional to take the load off your back.

PART SIX

Questions 41–52

- Read the text below about a company acquisition.

- In most of the lines **41–52** there is one extra word. It is either grammatically incorrect or does not fit in with the meaning of the text. Some lines, however, are correct.

- If a line is correct, write CORRECT on your Answer Sheet.

- If there is an extra word in the line, write the extra word in CAPITAL LETTERS on your Answer Sheet.

- The exercise begins with two examples (**0**) and (**00**).

Examples: **0** C O R R E C T

00 B E C A U S E

Evans cycles to a more active future

---

0   Active Private Equity has bought a majority stake in Evans Cycles,

00   because the independent chain of UK specialist cycling stores.

41   The retailer, which sells bicycles, accessories, clothing and their

42   services in its 31 stores, had reportedly been going in talks with

43   controversial sports billionaire, Mike Ashley, last summer and was said

44   to have such a price tag of around £35m. Yesterday, Active said it had

45   completed a refinancing of the group "to provide the necessary for

46   growth capital and expertise that will help the company fulfil its potential".

47   Despite the Smith Family has owned Evans for the past 50 years,

48   but they are thought to have wanted to reduce their holdings to a

49   minority stake. The company's turnover has doubled up over the last

50   three years to £45m. Nick Evans, who was introduced Active to the Evans

51   board, will take up the post that of executive chairman. Active partners Bryan

52   Vaniman and Spencer Skinner will also to join the Evans board as directors.

Writing

PART ONE

Question 1

- The bar charts below show working hours and production at two different sites of a company.
- Using the information from the charts, write a short **report** comparing the performance for the two sites.
- Write **120–140** words.

Average Working Hours

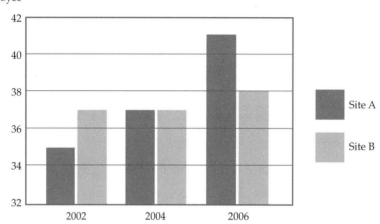

Units of Production

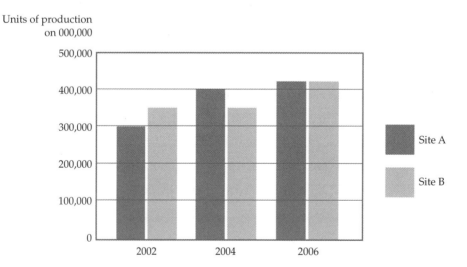

Before you write your answer to Part One, go on to pages 23–24.

Further Practice for Writing Part One

EXAM INFORMATION

In Part One of the Writing Test you have to produce a report of 120–140 words. In the report you will have to analyse graphic information and describe the information in writing. The graphic information can be in the form of line graphs, tables, bar charts or pie charts or a mixture. The instructions explain what the graphic information shows and ask you to describe or compare. The information may be about sales, production, costs, and other information found in company reports or the business pages in newspapers.

A DETAILED STUDY

1 *Put these words used to describe graphic information into the correct column below. Which word does not fit into any of the categories?*

rose	plunged	declined	levelled off	climbed	rallied
held	steadied	stabilised	crashed	recovered	soared
increased	dipped	bounced back	rocketed	fluctuated	decreased
flattened out	collapsed				

going up	going down	staying the same

2 *Which of the following adjectives can be used as intensifying adverbs in a report describing graphic information?*

surprising	sudden	general	rough	smooth	considerable
dramatic	slow	fast	significant	steady	fair
approximate	nice	virtual			

3 *Put the adverbs that you have created in exercise 2 into the correct columns. Can you add any more?*

Degree of change	Speed of change

4   *Put this advice about how to write a report on graphic information into the correct order.*

   1   Decide what the relationship is between the different types of information shown.

   2   Write the report, making sure you use a range of language.

   3   Look at the graphic information carefully and check you understand it.

   4   Check your writing for accuracy of spelling and grammar.

   5   Choose which points to include and in what order.

5   *Look at the graph below. Then look at the descriptions of the information in the graph and decide which one you think is best and why.*

Percentage change in exports

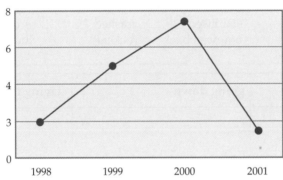

   1   In 1999 exports rose by 3%, in 2000 exports increased by 2.5% and in 2001 exports fell by 6%.

   2   After rising in 1999, exports continued to rise in 2000 but by a smaller percentage. They then dropped sharply in 2001 bringing them to below 1999 levels.

   3   Exports rose by 3% in 1999 and continued to rise in 2000 but by only 2.5%. Then in 2001 they dropped dramatically by 6%.

6   *Read this example of a report a student wrote to Part One on page 22. Then answer the questions below.*

   In 2002 both sites worked the shortest hours per week at 35 and 37. Then in 2004 they both worked 37 hours per week in average, which was good. In 2006 Site A jumped to working 41 hours per week and Site B rose slightly to 38 hours per week. In this time production at the sites changed. In 2002 it was 300,000 at Site A and 350,000 at Site B. In 2004 Site A rose by 100, 000 and Site B remaindered the same. In 2006 both sites made about 420,000.   (92 words)

   1   Is the report long enough?

   2   Does it follow the instructions?

   3   Which time phrase or reference is unclear?

   4   Can you find two language mistakes?

   5   The student has used some informal or subjective expressions in two places which are not appropriate. Can you find them and correct them?

Now write your own answer to Part One of the Writing Test. Remember to check for spelling and grammar mistakes.

PART TWO

Questions 2–4

- Write an answer to **one** of the questions 2–4 in this part.
- Write **200–250** words.

Question 2

- Your company is considering outsourcing the distribution of its products to another company. Your manager has asked you to write a report which assesses whether or not this is a good idea.
- Write the **report** for your manager:
- explaining what the benefits of outsourcing distribution will be
- describing what problems may occur as a result of this
- suggesting how easy it will be to find a suitable company to handle the distribution.

Question 3

- Your company is looking for an agent in another country which can help your company export its products or services. Your manager has asked you to write a letter to send to agents.
- Write the **letter** to the agents including the following information:
- what your company does
- why your company has decided to export
- what you will need an agent to do.

Question 4

- Your company is planning to change the way it advertises one of its products. Your manager has asked you to write a proposal suggesting new advertising methods.
- Write the **proposal** including the following information:
- what the problems are with the current method of advertising
- what new method of advertising you propose
- why you think your suggested method will be successful.

Listening

PART ONE

Questions 1–12

- You will hear a speaker talking to a group of trainee managers about project management.
- As you listen, for questions **1–12**, complete the notes using up to three words or a number.
- You will hear the recording twice.

How to manage a project

---

1   First, agree the so-called .... with your boss.

2   Fix break points when the .... of your project can be checked.

3   Select your team early so they can plan their .... to the project.

4   Install analytical software which includes a .... so you can check tasks are on schedule.

5   Possible problems with .... can be avoided by agreeing settlement dates in advance.

6   Having a .... will mean you can deal with any problems as they arise.

7   Give each member of staff a .... of what's required of them.

8   Try to assess how much .... each team member feels comfortable with.

9   A crucial part of motivation is .... and this applies to everyone.

10 Report significant information .... with your team members.

11 Make sure .... are maintained throughout in case complications arise later.

12 Once the project is complete, organise a .... session to discuss any issues.

Before you check your answers to Part One, go on to pages 27–28.

Further practice for Listening Part One

EXAM INFORMATION

In Part One of the listening test you hear an informational monologue twice. On your question paper, there is a gapped text with twelve spaces that you have to fill in with up to three words or a number. The gapped text may look like a series of notes or a form that is partly filled in.

The aim of this part of the test is to assess your ability to retrieve factual information. The answers are very specific and must be spelt correctly. The gapped text on the question paper does not replicate what the speaker says in the recording exactly, so you need to listen carefully and be prepared to reformulate some of what you hear.

A DETAILED STUDY

One way you can help yourself do better in this task is to try and predict what sort of answer is expected in each gap. Does the surrounding text indicate that the gap needs to be filled by, for example, a verb, an adjective, a noun, a number or a phrase? By working this out as you read through the text in the 45-second preparation time, you will be focused in on what the speaker is going to say.

INITIAL PREDICTION

Read these sentences and decide what type of word is missing.

1 Holding regular meetings helps staff .... what the company requires of them.

2 Focus on the .... of the job.

3 Well-known companies are often called ....

4 Last year inflation rose by............... .

5 The CEO introduced a .... programme of store renewals.

6 The going rate for the work is .... an hour.

7 Efficient .... is essential in this type of project.

8 Ensure that the security codes are .... every week.

It will help you more if you can narrow your predictions even further by, for example, deciding whether the verb is going to be singular or plural, present or past, infinitive or past participle. Similarly, you should try to predict whether a noun is going to be singular or plural. The type of number can be predicted too, for example, whether it is going to be a date, a cost or a percentage.

MORE DETAILED PREDICTION

Read these sentences and make a more detailed prediction of what should go in the gap.

1 Be prepared to reschedule if the .... are changed.

2 Companies need to .... their products to suit the changing market.

3 It wasn't until .... that he decided to set up his own business.

4 Insist on as much .... as possible.

5 The old warehouse is going to be .... by a new one next year.

6 An investment of no more than .... will get you access to the scheme.

7 There will be a .... of growth over the next few months.

8 It only took .... to find new premises.

9 We are looking forward to .... a new training programme.

10 I spoke to EAG's............... yesterday about the conference.

REFORMULATION

The information on the question paper will not be formulated in the same way as the information on the recording. This means you have to listen carefully and check for synonyms.

Question 1 on page 26 states:

First agree the so-called ... with your boss.

The speaker on the recording says:

it's essential to get your superior's approval for what you're planning, that means initially for what are referred to as 'the terms of reference'.

- 'boss' is equivalent to 'your superior'

- 'agree' is equivalent to 'approval'

- 'first' is equivalent to 'initially'

- 'the so-called' is equivalent to 'what are referred to as'

You can predict that you are looking for a noun, either singular or plural, to complete the gap, so that must be 'terms of reference'.

Go through the same analysis with Questions 4 and 11 on p26 and refer to the tapescript on page 152.

Question 4 on page 26 states:

Install analytical software which includes a ... so you can check tasks are on schedule.

- 'analytical software' is equivalent to ………………..……….. .

- 'individual tasks' is equivalent to …………………………………

- 'check' is equivalent to …………………………………….………….

The type of word required is………… so the answer is …………

Question 11 on page 26 states:

Make sure ... are maintained throughout in case complications arise later.

- 'are maintained' is equivalent to …………………………….. .

- 'in case complications arise later' is equivalent to …………………………

The type of word required is………… so the answer is …………

Now check your answers to these questions and look at your answers to Part One of the Listening Test.

PART TWO

Questions 13–22

- You will hear five people talking about a meeting they attended.

- For each extract there are two tasks. For Task One, decide which meeting each person attended from the list **A–H**. For Task Two, decide what meeting strategy each speaker recommends, from the list **A–H**.

- You will hear the recording twice.

TASK ONE – THE MEETING THEY ATTENDED

- For questions **13–17**, match the extracts with the meetings, listed **A–H**.

- For each extract choose the meeting each person attended.

- Write **one** letter (**A–H**) next to the number of the extract.

13 ....

14 ....

15 ....

16 ....

17 ....

    A company annual review

    B tender negotiation

    C training workshop

    D candidate selection

    E target setting

    F staff appraisal

    G team update

    H product development

TASK TWO – RECOMMENDED MEETING STRATEGY

- For questions **18–22**, match the extracts with the meeting strategy, listed **A–H**.

- For each extract, choose the main meeting strategy each speaker recommends.

- Write **one** letter (**A–H**) next to the number of the extract.

18 ....

19 ....

20 ....

21 ....

22 ....

    A prevent any participant from dominating

    B keep hand-outs to a minimum

    C establish a time limit for each section

    D deal with irrelevant contributions

    E read any material carefully before the meeting

    F ensure all members contribute

    G schedule items sensitively

    H summarise key decisions and action points

PART THREE

Questions 23–30

- You will hear a radio interview with an internet business coach about his career.
- For each question **23–30**, mark **one** letter (**A, B** or **C**) for the correct answer.
- You will hear the recording twice.

23 What was the main factor in Markus' decision to work in the financial sector?

    A He wanted to enter the same profession as his father.

    B He wanted to escape from an academic environment.

    C He thought the job would provide him with a real challenge.

24 Why does Markus refer to the suit he borrowed from his father?

    A to point out that the job he was doing was not right for him

    B to demonstrate how much he needed to earn his own money

    C to emphasise what an effort he made to adapt to the world of work

25 How does Markus view the ten years he spent working for finance companies?

    A He regrets the time he spent studying for his qualifications.

    B He thinks the fierce competition had a negative effect on him.

    C He realises that it was a process that he needed to go through.

26 Why did Markus decide to start his own business?

    A He felt he had nothing new to learn where he was.

    B He hoped that he would be able to earn a larger salary.

    C He wanted to use his work contacts for his own benefit.

27 What is innovative about Markus' business?

    A the topics he covers in his conference sessions

    B the centre he has for pre-business set-up queries

    C the advice he gives on ways to exploit the internet

28 What does Markus find difficult about working with the internet?

    A   persuading business entrepreneurs to use the social networking sites

    B   maintaining his interest in it now that it is a key feature of his work

    C   exploiting all the useful applications that are being developed

29 Markus believes that people who are considering setting up a business

    A   should make a priority of working out a detailed business plan.

    B   should aim to link something that appeals with a proven talent.

    C   should carry out detailed market research before doing anything else.

30 What advice about time does Markus offer top business people?

    A   It is very precious so use it in a way that is personally rewarding.

    B   Try to avoid staying at your desk beyond the normal working day.

    C   Make sure that what you receive reflects the hours spent on a project.

Speaking

PART ONE

Conversation between the examiner and each candidate (about 3 minutes)

In Part One of the Speaking Test, the interlocutor asks questions to each of the candidates in turn. You have to give information about yourself and express personal opinions.

Here are some questions you may be asked:

1   What type of work do you do?

2   What do you find most enjoyable about your work?

3   What training or study did you do before you started work?

4   What aspect of your work do you find most demanding?

5   What job would you like to be doing in five years' time?

6   How important is interacting with colleagues in your work?

7   How is technology changing the way people work in your country?

8   How important is English in businesses in your country?

9   How has the global market changed people's lives in your country?

Further practice for Speaking Part One

EXAM INFORMATION

The speaking test is taken in pairs (or threes when there is an extra candidate at the end of a session). There are two examiners. The interlocutor is the examiner who speaks to you and asks the questions. The other examiner observes and marks you. The interlocutor contributes to the marking process by awarding you one overall mark. You are awarded marks using the following criteria:

- grammatical resource
- lexical resource
- discourse management
- pronunciation
- interactive communication

PART ONE: THE INTERVIEW

In the first part of the speaking test, the examiner asks you questions about yourself, your work or studies and other personal matters. This lasts about three minutes and is designed to test your ability to talk about yourself and express personal opinions and preferences. You will be asked approximately the same number of questions as your partner, but not necessarily the same questions or in the same order. Listen carefully to the questions. Avoid giving one word answers or long prepared speeches. It is best if you can try to expand your answers beyond the bare minimum and link your ideas with words like 'because', 'so', 'but' .

Example: *Can you tell me a little about your job?*

Certainly. I work in the Sales department of an engineering company. My work involves contact with clients, so I travel quite a lot to visit different companies, which I enjoy very much.

A DETAILED STUDY

Below are responses to questions **3–9** on the previous page. Link each one of these to an appropriate extended response **A–H** using one of the words or phrases in the box (i –viii). There is one extra linking word or phrase which is not used.

1   I did an accountancy diploma

2   I find some of the statistics very hard to understand

3   I'd really like to work in our New York office for a while

4   It's very important

5   It's making some things much easier

6   It depends which business you are working in

7   It has made a huge difference to us

A   sending marketing information to thousands of potential clients

B   find out how they do business over there

C   nearly every company needs the language to some degree

D   I've never been good with figures

E   the work is done in teams as it is in my company

F   it has been very rewarding

G   in the area of exports

H   I found was a good preparation for a range of jobs

i in order to	**ii** for example	**iii** although	**iv** because	**v** if
vi so	**vii** especially	**viii** which		

PART TWO

Mini-presentation (about 6 minutes)

In this part of the test, you are asked to give a short talk on a business-related topic. You have to choose one of the topics from the three below and then talk for about one minute. You have one minute to prepare your ideas.

A: Sales: the importance of developing schemes to maintain customer loyalty

B: Training: the benefits to a company of encouraging staff to attend training courses

C: Operating systems: the factors involved in implementing change in a traditional organisation

When you have given your presentation, your partner will ask you a question about what you have said. Here are some questions they may ask you:

Can you explain what you meant by…?

Could you go into a bit more detail about…?

A • What kind of loyalty schemes could companies use?
  • Do you think loyalty schemes really increase business?
  • What do you think motivates customers more, discounts or gifts?

B • How can you ensure that training courses are worthwhile?
  • What business skills would it be particularly useful for staff to be trained in?
  • How would you deal with older staff members who do not want to do courses?

C • What should managers do to start the process of implementing change?
  • What research needs to be carried out before deciding on the changes?
  • What argument would you use to persuade staff of the need to introduce changes?

PART THREE

Discussion (about 7 minutes)

In this part of the test, you are given a discussion topic. You have 30 seconds to look at the prompt card and then about 3 minutes to discuss the topic with your partner. After that the examiner will ask you some more questions related to the topic.

For **two** candidates

Company Relocation

The company you work for is thinking of relocating to different premises outside the city. You have been asked to make some recommendations.

Discuss and decide together:

- *whether it would be better to move to an existing building or design a new one*
- *what the effects might be on staff of having to commute out of the city.*

For **three** candidates

Company Relocation

The company you work for is thinking of relocating to different premises outside the city. You have been asked to make some recommendations.

Discuss and decide together:

- *whether it would be better to move to an existing building or design a new one*
- *what the effects might be on staff of having to commute out of the city*
- *what benefits the new location might have on productivity.*

The examiner will then ask you some follow-up questions. Here are some questions you may be asked:

- What effect do you think a pleasant working environment has on motivation? (Why?)
- Should companies provide transport for staff if their premises are a long way from the nearest town? (Why? / Why not?)
- How far would you be willing to commute to work every day? (Why?)
- What are the advantages and disadvantages of working from home?

BEC TEST 2

Reading

PART ONE

Questions 1–8

- Look at the statements below and at the five extracts from an article on the opposite page about building effective teams in new companies.

- Which extract (**A, B, C, D** or **E**) does each statement (**1–8**) refer to?

- For each statement (**1–8**), mark one letter (**A, B, C, D** or **E**) on your Answer Sheet.

- You will need to use some of these letters more than once.

- There is an example at the beginning, (**0**).

1   The company owner should focus on fostering team spirit.

2   Individual members of staff should be allowed to negotiate their own terms.

3   Employees should be encouraged to experiment.

4   Staff are likely to leave if they can't keep up with what is required.

5   A system for assessing progress should be set up for staff.

6   A feature of new companies is that they are under-staffed.

7   Company owners should use external sources to help with some aspects of managing their team.

8   Employees can develop essential skills in new, expanding companies.

A

'Dream Team' people only have one characteristic – they get stuff done, rather than finding excellent excuses for inactivity. In every start-up there are many more jobs than people to do them. Also there is no time to have meetings to discuss strategies for solving problems; people have to just get on and do things. Often they'll screw up the first time, and that is quickly forgiven in a start-up so long as they don't keep making the same mistakes. It's easier to have a no-blame culture in a small organisation than a large one and people should be praised for 'having a go', even if the immediate consequences are less than ideal.

B

In a fast-growing company, nobody is interested in problems, only solutions, and the ability to execute quickly and bounce back swiftly from setbacks, is vital for personal and business survival in entrepreneurial companies. This is also the perfect learning experience for those who have dreams of themselves becoming a cornerstone one day or even of starting their own company.

C

Entrepreneurs attract ambitious people and, if left to their own devices, tend to hire in their own image so potential 'Dream Team' people are not difficult to identify. The problem is finding the ones that will fit in and deliver. My experience is that there is a strong element of 'natural selection' when entrepreneurs grow their organisations. There is rarely a formal recruitment or interview process, and if people do not shape up they tend to be out of the revolving door quite quickly.

D

Most important from the entrepreneur's point of view is to develop and maintain the right culture, which is essentially tribal. This should be actively encouraged and overlaid with a few minor elements of process and procedure. It's important to have formal, six monthly reviews with agreed targets, even if the playing field is changing on a daily basis. It's an opportunity for both parties, senior and junior to take a breath, try and make sense of what is happening and set some objectives for the next few months.

E

Remuneration is a tough issue and the wise entrepreneur gets advice and mentoring from people with specific expertise in the area, and who have been around the block several times. Then, the remuneration policy should be clearly and fairly executed, especially when shareholding or stock options are involved. There's nothing wrong with an ambitious employee coming to a manager and saying they should be paid as much as someone else, so long as they are willing to deliver as professionally and accept the same level of responsibility as the person they aspire to be.

PART TWO

Questions 9–14

- Read this article in which a company owner talks about her best deal.
- Choose the best sentence from the opposite page to fill each of the gaps.
- For each gap (**9–14**), mark one letter (**A–H**) on your Answer Sheet.
- Do not use any letter more than once.
- There is an example at the beginning, (**0**).

My Best Deal

It's not often that a television comedy programme can be credited with the beginning of a wonderful business relationship but for Sue Mitchells this is pretty much what happened. (**0**) ...H... Keeping a sales relationship long term can be challenging in the fast-moving world of the film production industry where there is typically rapid staff turnover and ever-changing technology.

Ms Mitchells, 38, is head of media client services for Ascent Media, a company that aims to be a one-stop shop for film and television production and employs 4,000 staff worldwide. (**9**) .... Her best deal came more than a decade ago when she was attending MIP TV, a conference in Cannes. (**10**) .... "I happened to bump into a client who I had known when I was at TVP, a company that was later bought by Ascent. She was moving to a new employer called VCI and suggested that I talk to the head of production there. (**11**) .... It is such a competitive industry that I'm sure she would have been receiving lots of other calls but fortunately my acquaintance said she would arrange a meeting between all three of us."

When the trio did get together, Ms Mitchells recalls, the old and new connections combined: "We got on really well, " she says. "I listened to the production head saying what she was doing and what her problems were." (**12**) ..... The work involved streaming and encoding some archived content on to DVDs. VCI was looking for help on the production front and Ms Mitchells said Ascent could do exactly that. "One of the first programmes we worked on was a comedy programme. We were basically repackaging content."

(**13**) ......". As her business changed, we informed the head of production how we could support her, " Ms Mitchells says. (**14**) "...... . This business will always be one that changes but this relationship has lasted the test of time. Having the same person still at the company, has enabled us to expand and develop through emerging technologies."

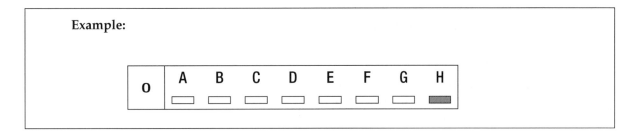

Example:

0	A	B	C	D	E	F	G	H
	☐	☐	☐	☐	☐	☐	☐	■

A She kindly agreed to give me some details of this lady.

B However, Ms Mitchells' relationship is still going strong.

C It turned out that VCI was doing a lot of work repackaging media content.

D She has worked for the group for 13 years, mostly in sales.

E One of the things that's been vital is that we spent a lot of time giving her company staff training and technical training because the industry changes rapidly with emerging technologies.

F This initial work went on and the relationship between the companies deepened. More than a decade later, they still work together.

G "The UK TV industry is a very social industry and everyone seems to know each other," she says.

H Winning some production work on archived material of a BBC comedy series for her company Ascent Media set in motion a connection that has now lasted more than a decade.

Before you check your answers to Part Two, go on to pages 40–41.

Further Practice for Reading Part Two

EXAM INFORMATION

Part Two of the Reading Test is a text with gaps where six sentences have been removed. You are given seven sentences to fill six of the gaps (one of the sentences is not needed). There is also an example. You have to match each gap with the sentence that fits both meaning and structure.

A DETAILED STUDY

The texts in this part always contain a line of thought or a narrative where one idea, fact or event is linked logically to the one before or after it. First, read the text and the sentences in order to understand the line of thought. Look for meaning, but also look out for single words and short phrases such as:

- pronouns, e.g. *it, their, him*

- demonstratives, e.g. *this, those*

- linking words and phrases, e.g. *However, In contrast, Additionally*

- comparisons, e.g. *better than, prefer* (one thing to another)

- referring nouns, e.g. *This situation/problem/issue/relationship*

Consider how they link one idea to another.

Also look for other elements of the text that demonstrate cohesion such as:

- A topic sentence summarising what is to come, e.g.

There can be several reasons why people do not always like travelling abroad on business. Managers should take employees' concerns on this issue seriously and investigate the reasons ... etc.

- A summary sentence followed by an example or explanation.

Saving costs in training can be achieved relatively simply. One way is to get employees to mentor each other ... etc.

1   *First try to understand the line of thought in the text. Read the article on page 38 and put the following in   order of when they are mentioned.*

    a   Ms Mitchells met a former client.

    b   VCI needed some help.

    c   A client set up a meeting for Ms Mitchells.

    d   Ms Mitchells trained staff at VCI.

    e   What Ms Mitchells does now.

    f   Ms Mitchells helped VCI.

    g   A former client gave Ms Mitchells useful contact details.

    h   Ms Mitchells met a former client and a new contact.

    i   Ms Mitchells went to Cannes.

2   *What do the words or phrases in italics in the following sentences refer to? They are all taken from the text.*

    1   ... for Sue Mitchells *this* is pretty much what happened.

    2   ... *where there* is typically rapid staff turnover ...

3 ... everyone seems to know each other, " *she* says.

4 *She* was moving to a new employer ...

5 ... I'm sure *she* would have been receiving lots of other calls ...

6 When *the trio* did get together ...

7 *The work* involved streaming and encoding ...

8 Ms Mitchells said Ascent could do exactly *that*.

3 *Match the two halves of these extracts by joining the underlined words and phrases to their reference. What other words help you to connect the extracts?*

1 Although I sympathise with the <u>situation</u>

2 <u>The director</u> wasn't in

3 This <u>issue</u> is

4 By running <u>sessions</u> at the same time

5 <u>Not everyone</u> is eligible.

6 It's excellent in <u>some</u> respects.

a we will be able to get through more

b However, we need to consider ...

c it cannot be allowed to continue

d Those who aren't should see me.

e so I spoke to his secretary.

f the problem which concerns me

4 *Now look at items A–G and answer the questions. This exercise helps you to relate the items to their proper place in the text. (Remember one item does not belong in the text). Remember you need to check any references after the gap as well as before the gap.*

A She kindly agreed to give me some details of this lady.

Who does *this lady* refer to?

B However, Ms Mitchells' relationship is still going strong.

What does *However* relate to?

C It turned out that VCI was doing a lot of work repackaging media content.

Which situation does *It turned out ...* refer to?

D Ms Mitchells, 38, is head of media client services for Ascent Media, a company that aims to be a one-stop shop for film and television production and employs 4,000 staff worldwide.

Is this sentence an introduction to someone or extra information about someone?

E This business will always be one that changes but this relationship has lasted the test of time.

What is *this relationship*?

F The initial work went on and the relationship between the companies deepened. More than a decade later, they still work together.

What kind of information would you expect to follow this sentence?

G "The UK TV industry is a very social industry and everyone seems to know each other," she says.

What kind of information would you expect to follow this sentence?

Now check your answers to these questions and look back at your answers to Part Two of the Reading Test.

PART THREE

Questions 15–20

- Read the following extract from an article about using customer magazines for marketing, and the questions on the opposite page.

- For each question (**15–20**), mark one letter (**A, B, C** or **D**) on your Answer Sheet for the answer you choose.

How magazines get goods into bags

1 As resistance to junk mail grows, big businesses are being forced to come up with ever-smarter ways to encourage their customers to spend more. Whether they are using customer
5 magazines, e-mails or podcasts, the name of the game for businesses is to get close to their clientele.

The sector that has benefited most from this shift is the contract-publishing sector, which
10 produces own-brand magazines for businesses. While traditional forms of print media are having a tough time, this segment is flourishing. "Traditionally, the holy grail for businesses was acquiring new customers. Now marketers
15 are realising that it is about nurturing existing customers. It is all about creating a dialogue with them, and that works in favour of customer magazines," says Julia Hutchison, chief operating officer of the Association of Publishing
20 Agencies (APA), the industry body for customer magazines.

The grand illusion of customer magazines is that they appear to be the opposite of junk mail – where the former are subtle and editorially
25 driven, the latter are crude and direct. This has lead to some detractors claiming that customer magazines are the marketing equivalent of the wolf in sheep's clothing – a cynical sales tool purporting to be a glossy magazine. Not so,
30 say the publishers. "Customers acknowledge that they are being sold to. Our research shows that they are savvy," says the APA's Hutchison. Recent APA research shows that such magazines lead to an average sales uplift of 8 per cent.

35 But, in spite of magazine boom, the sector is already moving on. The latest buzz word in the customer magazine market is "segmentation". This means that companies are slicing and dicing their databases and sending out specific
40 information to particular demographics of customer. Targeted e-mail spam, podcasts and micro-sites are set to become the next growth area. "More and more companies are realising that having got their websites up and running,

45 it is actually a pretty dead experience. The whole debate now is how we can get customers reading in a more exciting way," says Mark Jones, editorial director of Cedar.

So-called experiential marketing is widely
50 seen as the next big thing. The thinking is that consumers can no longer be pigeon-holed in definable age brackets or social classes, meaning that businesses must appeal to their attitudes, experiences and emotions. "Marketing has
55 moved beyond demographics", says Cedar's Jones. However some publishing executives believe that the sector is getting "carried away" with digital and experiential marketing. "We have spent the past two years proving the
60 success of customer magazines and, what, are we supposed to abandon ship now and say 'Well actually digital is the way forward?'," says John Brown's Hirsch.

One example of a company that is using its
65 customer data in a simple yet effective way is Tesco, the UK's largest retailer. Tesco has a database of 12m customers, all of whom use its Clubcard loyalty programme. Details of every single purchase have been collected, collated
70 and crunched by Dunnhumby, a data company. Although Tesco has a customer magazine, the vast amount of Dunnhumby's findings are used to identify shopping patterns and trends in Tesco's stores. This emphasis allows Tesco and
75 its suppliers to alter at short notice the mix of products that they offer to shoppers.

Tesco's rationale for obsessively focusing in on what is on its shelves is simple, says Edwina Dunn, who founded Dunnhumby. She says
80 that if shelves are stocked with exactly what customers want, there is less need for fancy promotions to entice them into stores. "The thing that everybody locks onto is communication with customers. Actually, that is not the most
85 important element. The key element is getting the ranges right in the stores. Getting those right means that customers will come back more," says Dunn. Perhaps it really is that simple, after all.

15 In the second paragraph, we learn that customer magazines have become a popular marketing technique because

   A   people no longer want to read traditional magazines.

   B   they offer a very direct form of communication.

   C   they are an effective way of getting new customers.

   D   new marketing techniques were needed in certain businesses.

16 What criticism do some people make of customer magazines?

   A   The articles are not as good as in traditional magazines.

   B   They only contain advertising material.

   C   They deceive customers into buying products.

   D   Customers should not be charged for them.

17 The fourth paragraph states that new developments will take place in order to

   A   direct marketing material at specific groups.

   B   increase customer interest in company magazines.

   C   deal with the fact that companies are updating their technology.

   D   make marketing material more engaging for customers.

18 According to the fifth paragraph some executives feel that experiential marketing

   A   should not replace other marketing methods.

   B   can take too long to research and set up.

   C   is only appropriate for digital marketing techniques.

   D   may be the best way of targeting customers according to age.

19 The writer introduces the example of the Tesco Clubcard in the sixth paragraph to show that

   A   information collected on the card can be used in the magazines.

   B   there are different ways of utilizing information from customers.

   C   some companies have a range of marketing methods.

   D   companies should respond quickly to customer needs.

20 What does Edwina Dunn say in the last paragraph?

   A   Retailers would like more communication with customers.

   B   Special promotions could increase customer numbers.

   C   Sales depend on product selection.

   D   Returning customers are more important than new customers.

PART FOUR

Questions 21–30

- Read the article below about starting a business.
- Choose the correct word to fill each gap from **A, B, C** or **D** on the opposite page.
- For each question **21–30**, mark one letter (**A, B, C** or **D**) on your Answer Sheet.
- There is an example at the beginning, **(0)**.

Adventures in micro-business

One in 10 adults would like to be their own **(0)**............ . But how easy is it to start your own business? What's difficult is making a new business sustainable, since more than half **(21)** .... within three years. So it's a really bad idea to quit your job and then start a business. Much better to start your own business first and then quit your job. But this doesn't necessarily mean that you need to start **(22)** .... Planning is an essential part of enterprise.

Step one is to plan exactly what you are going to sell. Step two is to calculate what it will cost to make the product or to **(23)** .... the service. Step three is to do market research to ensure that you will be able to sell enough to cover the costs. If your plans **(24)** .... that you can make a profit then you are in business.

In truth, step one is down to you. Think about how and why people will buy from you. And also consider the **(25)** .... needed to get them to buy (your marketing plan).

Step two is daunting but, luckily, there are **(26)** .... of help, of which the most obvious is an accountant. If funds don't permit the use of a professional **(27)** .... , then visit a bank to get their business start-up pack.

Step three is where you calculate what sales you'll need to make in order to **(28)** .... a profit. Only when you have satisfied yourself about the financial **(29)** .... of your business should you consider testing out your idea. Look to make initial sales to friends and family. Get as much **(30)** .... from customers as possible. And always be prepared to refine your offering.

Example:

    A executive   **B** chief   **C** head   **D** boss

0	A	B	C	D
	☐	☐	☐	▆

21 **A** fall   **B** subside   **C** fail   **D** resign

22 **A** handling   **B** trading   **C** establishing   **D** transacting

23 **A** consign   **B** execute   **C** fulfil   **D** deliver

24 **A** foresee   **B** predict   **C** forecast   **D** present

25 **A** advertisement   **B** promotion   **C** publication   **D** press

26 **A** representatives   **B** agents   **C** organisers   **D** sources

27 **A** adviser   **B** assistant   **C** counsellor   **D** backer

28 **A** generate   **B** create   **C** develop   **D** cause

29 **A** practicality   **B** worth   **C** benefit   **D** viability

30 **A** analysis   **B** talkback   **C** judgement   **D** feedback

PART FIVE

Questions 31–40

- Read the article below about working from home.
- For each question **31–40** write one word in CAPITAL LETTERS on your Answer Sheet.
- There is an example at the beginning, **(0)**.

Example: **0** | u | p | | | | | | |

Working from home carries a cost

If you set **(0)**.......... *an office in the spare bedroom, you need to talk to your insurer, warns Emma Lunn*

Most people dream of working from home **(31)** .... some point; no packed trains or traffic jams to contend with, merely the walk from your bedroom to the home office. Technology – **(32)** .... as broadband, home PCs and wi-fi – means that people can work effectively from home.

According **(33)** .... the Office of National Statistics, more than 2.1m people work from home and about 8m spend at **(34)** .... some of their working week in the house instead of an office. But, whether you are self-employed **(35)** .... teleworking for your employer, working from home comes **(36)** .... some financial implications. Being a homeworker throws up questions about insurance.

As **(37)** .... rule of thumb, people who work the odd day or two from home do not need to state that they use their home for business purposes, but if you work from home regularly, you will need to inform your insurer.

Debra Williams, managing director of insurance search engine Confused.com. says, "Some insurers will view people who work from home **(38)** .... a higher risk because expensive equipment may be kept **(39)** .... site, making it a potential target for thieves. Other insurers will take the view that people who work from home are **(40)** .... likely to be broken into as they are based in their house during the day."

Further practice and guidance for Reading Part Five

EXAM INFORMATION

Part Five consists of a text with eleven gaps. The first one is completed for you as an example. You have to supply **ONE** word to fill each gap. The focus is on grammatical structures and coherence/cohesion in the text. The kinds of words that are gapped may include:

- prepositions, e.g. *in, on, at*
- auxiliary verbs, e.g. *do, have, is*
- linking words, e.g. *however, so*
- articles, e.g. *a, the*
- relative pronouns, e.g. *who, which*
- conjunctions, e.g. *and, but, if*
- comparison words, e.g. *as, more*

A DETAILED STUDY

It is important to read through the passage first to get a clear idea of the meaning of the text as a whole. Before you select a word for the first gap, decide what type of word is needed e.g. an article, an auxiliary verb, a preposition etc. This will help you to focus on the structure of the sentence. If you do this, you will be more likely to choose the right type of word.

1   *Decide what type of word from the list above is needed in each of these gaps.*

   1   There are engineers .... are trained to do this kind of work.

   2   All the results .... been analysed.

   3   We'll need .... time than we calculated to finish the project.

   4   Working long hours is now .... norm for many managers.

   5   I need to get .... touch with the training manager.

   6   The deadline was yesterday, ... the building is still not complete

2   *A number of the questions in this task focus on common phrases. It is worth learning the most common by heart. Complete these phrases with one word only.*

   1   .... a result

   2   in .... words

   3   in terms ....

   4   that tends to be .... case

   5   not only .... also

   6   .... example

Now check your answers to these questions and look back at your answers to Part Five of the Reading Test.

PART SIX

Questions 41–52

- Read the text below about public relations.

- In most of the lines **41–52** there is one extra word. It is either grammatically incorrect or does not fit in with the meaning of the text. Some lines, however, are correct.

- If a line is correct, write **CORRECT** on your Answer Sheet.

- If there is an extra word in the line, write **the extra word** in CAPITALS on your Answer Sheet.

- The exercise begins with two examples (**0**) and (**00**).

Examples:

0	C	O	R	R	E	C	T	
00	F	O	R					

Get your message to the media

0   Public Relations is about perception management. You might run a great

00   company, your product or service might genuinely provide for great benefits,

41   but if the customer does not perceive it at that way, it remains on the shelves.

42   Consequently, among other tasks, executives must become

43   perception managers. To do this, they must integrate with public relations

44   into the company's total of communications mix. In coping with the media

45   there are two key rules. Know the media and the reporters that covering your

46   company. Decide who in your company should keep in touch with them.

47   Ordinarily, however, this will include a number of people. Not everyone in your

48   company is going to be as equally skilled at media relations, so pick those

49   with the knack. That can vary most according to the medium – print, TV

50   or internet. The company contact dealing with the media therefore may or

51   may not be the chief executive. Often companies will not want to make their

52   chief executives are available for interviews. But in the media age the chief

     executive's image is crucial to the success of the company he or she leads.

Writing

PART ONE

Question 1

- The charts below show sales at home and abroad for a company over a four-year period and changes in spending on advertising and marketing.

- Using the information from the charts, write a short **report** comparing sales with advertising and marketing spend during the four-year period.

- Write **120–140** words.

Sales at home and abroad

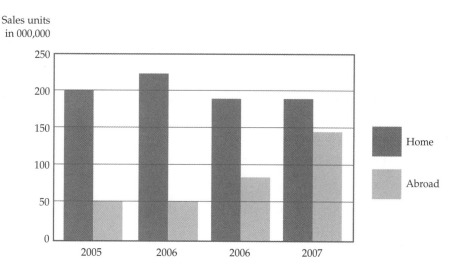

Spending on Advertising and Marketing

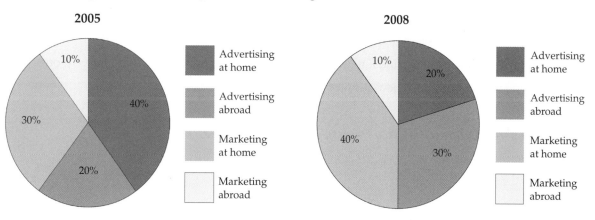

PART TWO

Questions 2–4

- Write an answer to **one** of the questions 2–4 in this part.
- Write **200–250** words.

Question 2

- Your company has recently put in place a programme to save energy and recycle waste. You have now been asked to write a report about how your department is progressing for the Managing Director.
- Write the **report** including the following information:
    - what measures your department took to save energy and recycle waste
    - how successful this programme has been
    - how you think the programme could be improved.

Question 3

- Your company is about to launch a new product or service. Your manager has asked you to write a letter to customers about the new product or service.
- Write the **letter** including the following information:
    - what the new product or service is
    - why the company decided to develop this product or service
    - why the customer should consider buying the product or service
    - what special deals you can offer.

Question 4

- Your company is not very happy with a supplier it is currently using. You have been asked to write a proposal for your Head of Department about this problem.
- Write the **proposal** for your Head of Department:
    - describing what the problems are with the current supplier
    - explaining why it is better to find a new supplier than resolve problems with the current one
    - suggesting ways of finding a new supplier.

Before you write your answer to Part Two (report), go on to pages 51–52.

Further practice for Writing Part Two (report)

EXAM INFORMATION

In Part Two of the Writing Test you have a choice of writing a report, a piece of business correspondence (e.g. a letter) or a proposal. You have to write between 200 and 250 words. Each task gives a reason for writing and says who the target reader is. There are specific bulleted instructions for each task to which you can apply your own knowledge and experience. In the tasks you have to address each content point using the appropriate range of language and register.

A DETAILED STUDY

1 *Which of these features would be appropriate for a report?*

　　1 headings

　　2 an introduction

　　3 a title

　　4 the writer's personal opinion

　　5 a recommendation

　　6 evidence to support statements

　　7 subjective language

2 *Which of these functions would you expect to see in a report? Note down an example of what is appropriate for each function you choose. The first one has been done for you.*

　　1 describing, e.g. a process, a system, a situation

　　2 explaining

　　3 persuading

　　4 suggesting

　　5 introducing

　　6 requesting

　　7 evaluating

3 *Which is the best sentence to open the report on page 50?*

　　1 Now I'm going to talk about the programme to save energy and recycle waste.

　　2 This report tells you about the programme for saving energy and waste that we have just put in place to see how successful it has been.

　　3 The aim of this report is to assess the success of the recent programme to save energy and recycle waste and to suggest what improvements could be made.

4 *Which sentence in each pair is more formal and why? The sentences relate to the task on page 50.*

　　1 a We decided to make sure that any copies we made used both sides of the paper.

　　　　b Staff were requested to ensure that they used both sides of the paper when making copies.

　　2 a The success of the programme is problematic to evaluate as the data is incomplete.

　　　　b Assessing the success of the programme is not easy as the data is incomplete.

3   a   The programme would be more successful if staff were reminded of what they should be doing through regular emails.

    b   I think the programme could be improved by sending regular emails to staff to remind them what to do.

5   *Rewrite the following in more formal language.*

1   gives

2   I think we should …

3   It worked well.

4   We put waste paper in a pile to use again.

5   … decided to set up a system …

6   *Read this extract from a report that a student wrote for Question 2 on page 50. Then decide which of the aspects listed could be improved and how.*

<u>What measures?</u>

Several measures were introduced. These included re-using printer ink cartridges, re-using waste paper for note taking and turning off lights in the middle of the day. These were all followed by all staff and the assistant manager checked to make sure everyone was doing as they were told. We were very happy with the results.

1   formality

2   range of language

3   focus

4   accuracy

5   layout

Now write your own answer to Part Two of the Writing Test. Remember to check for spelling and grammar mistakes.

Listening

PART ONE

Questions 1–12

- You will hear Matthew Brand, Marketing Manager of Magnum Optics, talking to a group of staff in his department about an upcoming trade fair.

- As you listen, for questions **1–12**, complete the notes using up to **three** words or a number.

- You will hear the recording twice.

Representing Magnum at the Eurotech trade fair

What happens before the fair

1 Some information on the company is included in the ....

2 A .... is set up in advance to check the outgoings.

3 Marketing items are carefully selected to provide a suitable .... of Magnum.

What to do at the fair

4 Remember to take a second .... in case of breakdown.

5 There will be a .... for every person on the stand.

6 It's important to take adequate .... in order to keep alert.

7 Remember to keep the literature at the .... of the stand.

8 Try to maintain .... as you talk to the visitors.

9 You can give visitors who are overloaded a .... with the logo on.

What happens after the fair

10 There will be a special .... when the fair closes to review everything.

11 Details are checked against the .... that were established beforehand.

12 All the .... that came out of the fair will need chasing up.

PART TWO

Questions 13–22

- You will hear five people talking about a marketing decision they made.

- For each extract there are two tasks. For Task One, decide what marketing strategy each person decided to adopt from the list **A–H**. For Task Two, decide what the main benefit of the strategy has been in each speaker's opinion, from the list **A–H**.

- You will hear the recording twice.

TASK ONE – MARKETING STRATEGY

- For questions **13–17**, match the extracts with the marketing strategy chosen by the speaker, listed **A–H**.

- For each extract decide on the appropriate marketing strategy.

- Write **one** letter (**A–H**) next to the number of the extract.

13	**A** direct mailing
	B point of sale displays
14	**C** website listing
	D a sponsorship deal
15	**E** a press release
	F special offers
16	**G** improved packaging
17	**H** a company newsletter

TASK TWO – MAIN BENEFIT

- For questions **18–22**, match the extracts with the main benefit of the marketing strategy, listed **A–H**.

- For each extract, choose the benefit each speaker describes.

- Write **one** letter (**A–H**) next to the number of the extract.

18	**A** The average age of customers on our database decreased.
	B The product information reached the public at the right time.
19	**C** People were more willing to believe that the information was correct.
20	**D** The products lost their exclusive image.
	E Customers found the information was much clearer than before.
21	**F** Customers thought the quality of the product ingredients had improved.
22	**G** People took more time to consider the product range.
	H People recommended the products to their friends.

Before you check your answers for Part Two, go on to pages 55–56.

Further Practice for Listening Part Two

EXAM INFORMATION

In Part Two of the Listening Test you hear five short monologues which are linked by a theme or a topic. The monologues are spoken by five different people. On the question paper there are two lists of eight options, which relate to the content and purpose of the monologues. Your task is to match what each speaker says with one of the options on each list.

You will hear the recordings twice and you must attempt both tasks during this time. You can decide whether you do the first task while you listen to the recording for the first time and the second task during the second listening or whether you prefer to deal with the two tasks for each monologue together. It is a good idea to try out both methods and decide which suits you best.

The aim of this part of the test is to assess your ability to identify context, topic, function and speaker's opinion etc. These will not be stated directly so you are being tested on your ability to infer meaning.

A DETAILED STUDY

The options on the question paper will not be expressed in the same way as they are in the recordings. Other options will also be mentioned in order to distract you. It is useful to recognize how this reformulation and 'distraction' works so that you can avoid making the wrong choices.

*Do these exercises **after** you have completed the task on the previous page, but **before** you check the answers.*

REFORMULATION

Underline in the tapescript the words which tell you what the answers are to Task One and Task Two, that is, what marketing strategy Speaker 1 chose and what benefit she describes.

Speaker 1

Sales declined last year so we decided to change the marketing mix. We held a brainstorming session and some people suggested sending out a mailshot in specific regions with a money-off coupon. That can have a very positive effect, though it tends to be short-term. Another more radical suggestion was to look at how the product range was presented, you know, colour of the wrapping, visuals, type of print and so on. After some thought we suggested that and management agreed. Sales rose and when we asked customers for their views, surprisingly, over 60% of respondents thought the sauces tasted different and suspected we'd used real tomatoes instead of tomato flavouring. So what we'd intended to do, which was just create a younger more 'fun' image, had a different and much wider-reaching effect.

DISTRACTION

1   *Now look at the tapescript for Speaker 1 again and underline any information which refers to other options in Task One.*

2   *Now look at the tapescript again and underline any information which refers to any other options in Task Two.*

3   *Now complete the same procedure with the tapescript for Speaker 4.*

Speaker 4

A new employee suggested an idea. I expected it to be internet-related – not that I'm against that. Lots of sales come through our website and our presence on web directories. No, her idea was that customers would buy more if they sat down and really examined what we offered carefully. When we tried out her proposal, sales did increase and a telephone survey revealed that was the reason. She believes people only glance at publicity offers sent by companies they use, however much they improve the way products are presented, because there's so much junk mail nowadays. However, if they receive a communication regularly, filled with information about changes in the firm and tips related to the products – in our case gardening hints – they'll pay attention and it builds customer loyalty.

4   *Finally, underline the words in the Speaker 4 tapescript that indicate that Task One options C and A are not correct.*

Now check your answers to these questions and look at your answers to Part Two of the Listening Test.

PART THREE

Questions 23–30

- You will hear a junior manager, Julia, discussing an MBA assignment with a senior colleague, Frank.

- For each question **23–30**, mark **one** letter (**A, B** or **C**) for the correct answer.

- You will hear the recording twice.

23 According to Frank, the main reason for a planned change failing is

    A   an underlying problem in the company structure.

    B   a lack of belief among staff in the actual need for it.

    C   an underestimation of the time needed to achieve it.

24 Frank and Julia agree that Julia's former boss

    A   probably didn't value the staff's intelligence enough.

    B   may have been trying to protect the staff from worry.

    C   should have told the staff why the changes were needed.

25 Frank thinks that the people who deal with change best are those who

    A   have an imaginative approach.

    B   do their jobs very efficiently.

    C   are willing to be flexible.

26 What does Frank consider is hard about transforming a whole business?

    A   People have to get used to a whole series of changes.

    B   It may involve having to give up what the company did best.

    C   Persuading staff that it is worth working hard to achieve the new goal.

27 What is Julia's opinion of the way managers communicate change to their staff?

    A   They need to support their words with practical measures.

    B   They should prepare their formal speeches more carefully.

    C   They spend too long discussing the issues with other directors.

28 What point does Frank's story about the sun and the wind illustrate?

  A   It is sometimes useful to explain difficult ideas with basic images.

  B   The best way is to persuade people of the value of a proposed change.

  C   Management have the power to enforce change but it may be painful.

29 What aspect of the MBA course is Julia most impressed by?

  A   the relevance of the course materials

  B   the friendliness of the teaching staff

  C   the calibre of the other students

30 What do Julia and Frank agree is the greatest benefit of doing an MBA course?

  A   increasing knowledge through reading

  B   having time to think about issues

  C   meeting influential people

Speaking

PART ONE

Conversation between the examiner and each candidate (about 3 minutes)

In Part One of the Speaking Test, the interlocutor asks questions to each of the candidates in turn. You have to give information about yourself and express personal opinions.

Here are some questions you may be asked:

1 What are you studying / did you study?

2 Why did you choose this subject?

3 What do / did you like most about your studies?

4 What is / was most challenging on your course?

5 How important is English in business studies in your country today?

6 What is the advantage of studying at university in another country?

7 What aspect of your course do you think will be most helpful in your future life?

8 What effect do you think technology is having on education in your country?

9 How important do you think studying business is for the future of your country?

10 What are your main ambitions for the future?

PART TWO

Mini-presentation (about 6 minutes)

In this part of the test, you are asked to give a short talk on a business-related topic. You have to choose one of the topics from the three below and then talk for about one minute. You have one minute to prepare your ideas.

> **A: Recruitment:** how to prepare appropriately before interviewing a selection of job applicants

> **B: Distribution:** the importance of ensuring that goods reach the purchasers on time

> **C: Company structure:** the benefits to an organisation of employees working together in teams

When you have given your presentation, your partner will ask you a question about what you have said. Here are some questions they may ask you:

Can you explain what you meant by…?

Could you go into a bit more detail about…?

A • **What kinds of question provide most information to interviewers?**

  • How useful is it to ask applicants to complete work-based tasks?

  • Do you think a panel of interviewers is better than one interviewer?

B • **What steps can you take to make sure that deliveries are not delayed?**

  • Should companies keep large stocks to avoid disappointing customers?

  • What compensation should you offer customers if goods are delayed?

C • **How do you feel personally about working in a team?**

  • What are the qualities of a good team member?

  • Does team work suit all kinds of business operation?

Before you give your answer to Part Two, go on to page 61.

Further practice for Speaking Part Two

EXAM INFORMATION

Part Two – The mini-presentation

In the second part of the speaking test, you have to give a mini-presentation on a business topic. You have a choice of three topics. You have one minute to prepare your presentation and the presentation itself should last about one minute. When you have finished the other candidate will ask you one or two questions about what you have said.

This part of the test is designed to see how well you organize more extended speech. You are expected not only to give information about the topic, but to express your opinion, justify your point of view and give examples from your own experience where relevant.

A DETAILED STUDY

Preparation

Success in this part of the test depends on using your one-minute preparation time well. The first thing to do is to choose your topic wisely. Select the one that you have most experience or information about as it will be easier if you can talk about something that is relevant to you. For example, if you have recently had an interview for a job, choose topic A. It is also important to choose a topic which you have some appropriate vocabulary for. Remember that topic A is the most general one and topic C is the most specialised one. It is perhaps wise, therefore, to avoid topic C unless you are familiar with the area of business it targets.

People prepare in different ways. Try these different methods and decide which suits you best:

- Write headings for the main points you will cover with subpoints/examples underneath
- Draw a mind map with the topic in the centre and key information coming out from it
- Use the time to plan the main points in your head but don't write anything down.

Introduction

Your presentation will sound more professional if you start with a brief introduction.

Complete these introductory sentences.

1   I'd like to talk ………. interviewing job applicants.

2   I'm going to start …. considering the number of interviewers.

3   Then I'd like to ……….. on to the venue.

4   And to ……… I'm going to mention interview tasks.

Expressing your ideas

At this level, examiners are looking for candidates who can produce a range of structures and appropriate expressions and use them accurately. When you are preparing for the test, listen critically to how you structure your presentation and try to avoid starting sentences in the same way, for example with 'I think'... .

For topic C, match each phrase in **1–7** *with a phrase in* **a–g** *to make a complete sentence.*

1	Personally, I always try to	**a)**	an opportunity to brainstorm ideas.
2	What I find helpful is having	**b)**	the way staff feel about teams.
3	In my view, it also benefits the company by	**c)**	everyone has different strengths.
4	It's worth bearing in mind that	**d)**	get to know my team socially.
5	In addition companies shouldn't overlook	**e)**	ensuring plans are fully checked.
6	I would also say that teamwork helps	**f)**	they risk wasting a lot of time.
7	If companies don't introduce teamwork then	**g)**	to speed up the design process.

Now check your answers to these questions and go back to Part Two of the Speaking Test.

PART THREE

Discussion (about 7 minutes)

In this part of the test, you are given a discussion topic. You have 30 seconds to look at the prompt card and then about 3 minutes to discuss the topic with your partner. After that the examiner will ask you some more questions related to the topic.

For **two** candidates

Advertising project

The toy company you work for is keen to advertise its new range of educational toys. You have been asked to make recommendations about the best ways to do this.

Discuss and decide together:

- *how to select an appropriate advertising medium for the target audience*
- *how to ensure that the company gets value for money*

For **three** candidates

Advertising project

The toy company you work for is keen to advertise its new range of educational toys. You have been asked to make recommendations about the best ways to do this.

Discuss and decide together:

- *how to select an appropriate advertising medium for the target audience*
- *how to ensure that the company gets value for money*
- *how to analyse the results of the advertising campaign*

The examiner will then ask you some follow-up questions. Here are some questions you may be asked:

- Do you think the benefits of advertising on TV are overrated? Why? / Why not?
- What are the benefits of using a well-known advertising agency?
- Would you agree that the best form of advertising is personal recommendation?
- Do you think companies should pay celebrities to endorse their products? Why? / Why not?

Reading

PART ONE

Questions 1–8

- Look at the statements below and at the five extracts from an article on the opposite page about some research into the causes of conflict between companies and their suppliers.
- Which extract (**A, B, C, D** or **E**) does each statement (**1–8**) refer to?
- For each statement (**1–8**), mark one letter (**A, B, C, D** or **E**) on your Answer Sheet.
- You will need to use some of these letters more than once.
- There is an example at the beginning, (**0**).

Example:

    0   Projects can be saved by having key staff who think positively.

---

1   Companies need to make certain that senior staff are committed to a project.

2   Teams may complete work as expected but with varied goals.

3   The success of a project may depend on the skills of key staff.

4   Staff need to be persuaded by the reasons behind any decisions.

5   Good communication between different layers of staff cannot be assumed.

6   Diverging objectives can be resolved by having a clear system in place.

7   Projects can fail because the people involved are not honest with each other.

8   Staff become more involved when they share information with the other company.

Andreas Brinkhoff and Ulrich Thonemann have researched supply chains for three years and found that the majority achieve less than expected.

A

The first factor is that of insufficiently clear goals or insufficient agreement with the other partners. This problem was present in 58% of the failures. In some cases, the teams actually performed as planned, but went off in different directions. Philipp Karallus, who heads the e-business centre of Bayer Material Sciences, found that this problem created enormous difficulties in the supply chain logistics. Fortunately, this was solved early on in the process, through a very consistent and well-communicated standardisation of packaging and quantities.

B

The people who actually work on the project must be convinced that any planned changes are necessary and appropriate. In 75% of the failures, the employees directly affected were not fully behind the project. Supply-chain manager Jeremy Bentham of plastics manufacturer Borealis found that joint workshops, including both firms, provide a good solution. These entail not only communication on all elements of the project, but ensure the mutual development of change. This regular exchange of ideas also works wonders for motivation.

C

Top management support is vital in order to ensure that the necessary resources are provided. Yet, such support is by no means the rule and two thirds of failures were attributable to this shortcoming. However, a project between 3M Healthcare and a large clinic is one example of where it did succeed. Ulrich Gellings, head of customer service at 3M in Germany, said that "the whole thing worked because the managers of both enterprises were clearly and genuinely behind the project and its objectives". But he explained that this kind of positive interaction between project and line management can never be taken for granted.

D

As with any relationship, people must feel free to talk openly about problems in order to find solutions. Of the failed projects, just over half were plagued by a lack of trust. As the manager of a Dutch chemical concern pointed out: "Whether or not the whole thing works will ultimately depend on the relationships involved." Specifically, where there is a lack of trust, the participants often spend more time haggling over contracts than they do on the actual work. The inevitable lack of transparency and concealment that accompanies such relationships, generally leads to the collapse of the project.

E

The effectiveness of the project leaders constitutes factor number five. Given the time span and organisational separation of the partners, such leadership is fundamental. These leaders form the interface between project teams and have to cope with problems from both sides. They have to be excellent communicators and motivators, not an easy task in complex projects where the contribution of the individual to the whole is not always particularly clear. Brinkhoff and Thonemann found that managers' willingness and ability to approach and resolve conflicts constructively proved indispensable.

PART TWO

Questions 9–14

- Read this text taken from an article about whether training is important for managers.
- Choose the best sentence from the opposite page to fill each of the gaps.
- For each gap (9–14), mark one letter (A–H) on your Answer Sheet.
- Do not use any letter more than once.
- There is an example at the beginning, (0).

Are managers born or made?

There seems to be much more debate on this question than about whether sales people are born or made, or whether writers are. Why is that? (0) ..H.. .

This month, the Chartered Institute of Personnel and Development (CIPD) released a report, which suggests that the lower level of productivity in the UK in comparison with the United States can be attributed, at least in part, to the poor level of people management in our companies. John Philpott, the CIPD's chief economist, argued that companies weren't doing enough to improve management standards. "One of the problems is the tradition which holds that good management comes out of the ether - that people either have it or they don't," he said. (9) " ..... ." Philpott's comments probably reveal a common frustration among training companies. One of the reasons some potential clients give for not purchasing management development programmes is that there would be little point, because managers are born and can't be made. (10) ..... . People only excel at things they enjoy doing and very few people honestly do want to manage others. Dealing with people every day is extremely demanding. (11) ..... . The ability to read other people accurately is certainly not common, and is surely unlearnable.

Management training too often attempts to shut the stable door after the horse has already bolted and is causing havoc. (12) ..... . If managers were asked to concentrate exclusively or predominantly on managing people, and their pay depended only on the performance of their team, you would immediately see management standards improve. (13) .... Under this system, you would have to really want to manage.

Few companies would currently wish to contemplate such a fundamental change. (14) ..... . In fact, management training should wait until there is something to work with. Let's first arrange some education for senior executives in the importance of good managers and some training in how to find and use them.

Example:

A What is first required is a profound structural change in selecting managers and then in how they are deployed and rewarded.

B The view is that management training certainly has an important role in developing further the managers who have it but the ones who don't are a lost cause.

C It is therefore far easier to offer them management training courses predicated on the myth that you can make all those bad managers good.

D Any ambitious individual who wants to ascend the corporate ladder almost always has to take on a management role first.

E To manage individuals properly, you have to be able to identify their strengths and potential quickly and discover exactly how to talk and act with them to encourage them to work harder and better.

F But there's a lot of evidence to suggest that you can learn to be a good manager and there are particular practices you can put in place.

G Not only because managers would be focused on managing people well, but also because much better managerial candidates would put themselves forward in the first place.

H And more importantly, what's the answer to the question in the first place?

PART THREE

Questions 15–20

- Read the following extract from an article about improving the innovation process, and the questions on the opposite page.

- For each question (**15–20**), mark one letter (**A, B, C** or **D**) on your Answer Sheet for the answer you choose.

A little anarchy at work can do a world of good

Coming up with new products and new ways of operating is necessary to ensure the survival of both individual firms and entire industries. But there remains considerable uncertainty as to why so many newly introduced products – estimates range up to 50 per cent – flop.

The reason for innovation glitches, according to recent research at the University of Bochum, in Germany, are rigid businesses structures and organisation. As soon as there is talk of innovation, people get nervous about their own position, so many managers delay or limit their co-operation. Many are unable to adapt to new technology and compatibility problems lead to high costs. Firms also have little or no experience with new technology and the external market is generally underdeveloped. As a result, clients' willingness to buy innovative goods or services is often incorrectly estimated. So, the research concludes, the insufficient integration of personnel, organisational, technical and client-related processes, leads to the high flop rate.

So far, no innovation process model has proven fully satisfactory, particularly for radical innovations. A recent and wide-ranging study conducted by Professor Cornelius Herstatt and his colleagues at the University of Hamburg attempted to solve the problems in their own innovative way. The research focuses on the benefits of optimising the early innovation phases. The Hamburg group believes the vital initial phases of the innovation process have been neglected in both theory and practice.

Yet, this so-called "fuzzy front-end" is where the foundations of the innovation process are laid. Early co-operation between the different disciplines in a business does much to reduce later tensions and misunderstanding. A targeted reduction of technical and market uncertainty from the beginning further increases the chances of success. Costs and resource needs are specified as clearly as possible to establish what can be achieved and whether plans are practicable. In order to ensure internal support, people need to be convinced, and realistically so, of the real value of products and projects.

The Bochum team, led by Professor Kriegesmann, stress that, in many enterprises, managers believe that a systematic analysis of competitors and clients, together with traditional planning processes, provides a sound basis for innovation. This is often not the case. Prof. Kriegesmann believes in "partisan wars" in which small groups within the firm develop innovative ideas contrary to the mainstream. In other words, successful innovation is frequently the result, not of central planning, but of trial and error and the learning processes of groups of innovators given the freedom to operate as independent units.

Implementation of even the finest concepts often fails unless initiatives are made very specific and tested over time in the market, possibly several times, until they are exactly what the customer wants. This requires a high level of commitment and a lot of work – precisely what these small groups of dynamic "partisans" do so well. They often go "underground" in companies and only emerge when they are convinced of success. It is, therefore, individuals or small groups working in their own special way that really deliver the innovative goods.

Particularly in old and possibly over-developed organisations, these relatively free-thinking and highly active groups may be the only way to innovate beyond prevailing trends and fashions. This gives progressive firms a new way to move forward by encouraging change-oriented forces inside the company.

15 Bochum University discovered that the high percentage of failure in innovations is caused by

    A customers' reluctance to change.

    B the limited investment in new technology.

    C a lack of flexibility in the costing system.

    D a lack of co-ordination between sections in a company.

16 In the third paragraph researchers at the University of Hamburg claim that

    A radical innovations require different processes.

    B an original approach to fostering innovation has failed.

    C previous research has failed to address a key area of innovation.

    D it is beneficial to separate innovation into different phases.

17 In the fourth paragraph the writer says that innovation is successful when

    A staff can see that the innovation will increase profits.

    B good communication is used to resolve problems that occur.

    C budgets are generous enough to allow risks to be taken.

    D projects are begun in good time to meet market needs.

18 What does the Bochum team believe about innovation?

    A Current managers have inadequate training in innovation.

    B Experimentation is an important part of innovation.

    C Risks can be reduced if smaller groups are used to innovate.

    D Groups working on innovation need an effective plan.

19 What does the writer suggest about the way that 'partisans' operate?

    A They have to use a variety of processes to reach a solution.

    B They usually have to work in the evenings and at weekends.

    C They work best when they are in a different location from the rest of the company.

    D They usually only produce solutions that they know will work.

20 What is the main point in this article?

    A Too many innovative products are failing.

    B Innovation should be incorporated into normal company processes.

    C Companies should rethink how they approach innovation.

    D We know very little about the process of successful innovation.

Before you check your answers to Part Three, go on to pages 70–71.

Further practice for Reading Part Three

EXAM INFORMATION

Part Three of the Reading Test is a text accompanied by four-option multiple choice items. The initial part of the multiple choice item – the stem – may be a question or an incomplete sentence. There are six questions and usually the questions test opinion or inference rather than straightforward facts.

A DETAILED STUDY

1   *First, read the text to get an understanding of the topic and the argument or overall opinion expressed. Read the text on page 68 and match each paragraph to the topics listed below.*

   1   how to focus on the beginning of the innovation process

   2   the causes of the problems

   3   why a radical solution works

   4   introduction to topic

   5   where the solution will be particularly effective

   6   a solution which differs from mainstream thinking

   7   the history of a solution which focuses on the beginning of the innovation process

2   *Now you need to locate the appropriate piece of text for the answer. Read only the stems for each question and underline the words in the text that reflect the stem. Remember the text may paraphrase the stem.*

3   *Try not to get confused by the options for each question. Read the text again then try to answer each question WITHOUT looking at the options. Cover the options then look at the text and the question together and make notes.*

4   *Often the options will not be worded the same as the text but will use paraphrases. Find paraphrases in the text for these words:*

   1   lack of co-ordination (paragraph 2)

   2   failed to address (3)

   3   staff can see (4)

   4   profits (4)

   5   experimentation (5)

   6   left to their own devices (5 and 6)

5   *When working with texts, you can expand your vocabulary by word building. This means that you can look up words in your dictionary and find other words related to them, e.g. co-operate (verb), co-operation (noun), co-operative (adjective).*

Complete the following tables. All the words are taken from the text.

noun	verb	adjective	negative	
1	2	introduced	x	
3	adapt	4	x	
compatability	x	5	6	(adj)
willingness	7	8	9	(vb/adj)
10	prove	11	12	(adj)
13	solve	14	15	(adj)
16	17	targeted	x	
18	19	specified	20	(adj)
21	develop	22	23	(vb/adj)
24	x	dynamic	25	(adj)

6   *You can also expand your vocabulary by checking you know the meaning of any words and expressions you are unfamiliar with. Match items 1–8 to the definitions A–H.*

1   coming up with (line 1)

2   flop (line 6 & 22)

3   glitches (line 7)

4   optimising (line 29)

5   disciplines (line 36)

6   sound (line 50)

7   go underground (line 66)

8   prevailing (line 74)

A   improving the way that something is done or used

B   sensible and likely to produce the right results

C   existing or accepted

D   thinking of a new idea or plan

E   small faults in a machine or process

F   do something secretly

G   areas of knowledge

H   fail

Now check your answers to these questions and look back at your answers to Part Three of the Reading Test.

PART FOUR

Questions 21–30

- Read the article below about a supermarket expansion plan.

- Choose the correct word to fill each gap from **A, B, C** or **D** on the opposite page.

- For each question **21–30**, mark one letter (**A, B, C** or **D**) on your Answer Sheet.

- There is an example at the beginning, (**0**).

Asda creating 3,900 jobs in expansion drive

Supermarket group Asda is to create 3,900 new jobs (**0**) ..C... the UK by the end of the year in a £360 million expansion (**21**) ..... , the company has announced. The chain, which is owned by US retail (**22**) ...... Wal-Mart, has received planning permission for seven new branches and the relocation of a further three existing stores, as well as the extension of five sites already (**23**) ..... operation. Part of the store extension plans includes adding 'mezzanine' floors in the loft spaces of existing outlets where strict planning regulations (**24**) ..... expanding the building outwards. The strategy, (**25**) ..... in York, involves moving goods to secure marquees in the car park so that the supermarket can continue to (**26**) ..... while it is converted to have an extra floor – a process which takes about three months.

Asda supermarkets in Sheffield and Wigan are to be converted into 'supercentres' selling a broader (**27**) ..... of products, including sports equipment or even furniture, creating 300 new jobs between them. Another 300 jobs will be (**28**) ..... by ploughing £38 million into extending several branches. The £25 million relocation of a store in Bournemouth is set to create another 150 jobs. The company expects to (**29**) ..... two of a further three relocations by the end of this year (**30**) ..... sites at Widnes, Cheshire and Edinburgh, both of which are set to create 150 new jobs, and in Halifax, where 100 positions are planned.

Example:

   A over   **B** along   **C** across   **D** among

0	A	B	C	D
	☐	☐	▭	☐

21 **A** action   **B** drive   **C** advance   **D** surge

22 **A** colossus   **B** monster   **C** giant   **D** body

23 **A** in   **B** at   **C** on   **D** into

24 **A** avoid   **B** check   **C** restrain   **D** prevent

25 **A** proved   **B** experimented   **C** piloted   **D** examined

26 **A** trade   **B** deal   **C** transact   **D** traffic

27 **A** class   **B** range   **C** series   **D** chain

28 **A** generated   **B** caused   **C** formulated   **D** initiated

29 **A** achieve   **B** perform   **C** settle   **D** complete

30 **A** containing   **B** concerning   **C** involving   **D** covering

PART FIVE

Questions 31–40

- Read the article below about cultural differences.
- For each question **31–40** write one word in CAPITAL LETTERS on your Answer Sheet.
- There is an example at the beginning, **(0)**.

Example: | **0** | S | O | M | E | | | | |

Culture lessons

One thing that a lot of companies overlook when they expand abroad is to provide their employees with **(0)** ….. sort of training in the way things are done in the countries which the company is going to export **(31)** ……. . Usually, senior executives visit the country and arrange matters with agents there, or it may **(32)** ….. that a production unit is set up in another country. In doing **(33)** ….., they expect to be able to export the 'way they do things', along **(34)** ….. the product, rather than trying to adapt to the local business culture. There can then follow months or even years of frustration and delays during **(35)** ….. everybody works out what is going on. It would be much faster, and therefore much cheaper, **(36)** ….. companies invested in 'culture' training so that everybody was fully prepared.

(37) ….. is strange is that companies are quite prepared to recognise cultural differences between companies within a country and to put steps in place to deal with those differences, for example, following a takeover. Yet, there often seems to be an assumption **(38)** ….., when the company takes its products and services abroad, the market will be so glad to receive them that cultural issues will **(39)** ….. stand in the way. Smaller companies should take a leaf out of the book of the multinationals, who are well-versed in cultural differences and address the issue head on, so that it benefits, rather than detracts **(40)** ….., the bottom line.

PART SIX

Questions 41–52

- Read the text below about how to dress at work.

- In most of the lines **41–52** there is one extra word. It is either grammatically incorrect or does not fit in with the meaning of the text. Some lines, however, are correct.

- If a line is correct, write CORRECT on your Answer Sheet.

- If there is an extra word in the line, write the extra word in CAPITALS on your Answer Sheet.

- The exercise begins with two examples (**0**) and (**00**).

Examples:

0	C	O	R	R	E	C	T	
00	F	O	R					

Dress for success

---

  0 Most people realise that they have to dress reasonably smartly when

 00 they are attending for an interview. They know that their job may

 41 depend on the impression the interviewers have of them by looking

 42 at their clothes. However, once they have had the job most people

 43 settle into just wearing comfortable clothes and so getting on with

 44 their work. If you want to be promoted, this is definitely not the

 45 way you should think! Research shows that people who considered to

 46 be the most suitable for promotion take two such important factors

 47 into account when they choose what to wear. Firstly, they are dress to

 48 fit in the company image. So, if dark suits are the norm, then they wear

 49 dark suits. If it's a young, dynamic company where the creativity is

 50 important then they may wear brighter or more than individual clothes.

 51 Secondly, they dress the same as the managers above them so, in this

 52 way, that they begin to be thought of as management material themselves.

 The message is – if you want to get ahead, dress as if you are already there!

Before you check your answers to Part Six, go on to page 76.

Further practice for Reading Part Six

EXAM INFORMATION

In Part Six of the Reading Test you are asked to read a short text and identify extra words which should not be there. The text contains twelve numbered lines which are the test items. Any lines which are not numbered are there to complete the text but are not test items. Some of the test lines will be correct, i.e. there will be no error.

The extra words are often words such as:

- pronouns, e.g. *it, they*
- prepositions and particles, e.g. *of, at*
- definers, e.g. *the, a, some, any, each*
- adverbs, e.g. *so, too, very*
- verb forms, e.g. *will, is, got*
- linking words, e.g. *despite*

A DETAILED STUDY

1 *To get a general understanding, read the text on page 75 and answer the following questions.*

   1 Why do people dress smartly for an interview?

   2 What do many people do once they start a job?

   3 What kind of people are considered for promotion?

   4 What two factors do such people take into account when they are dressing for work?

   5 What is the main message of the text?

2 *Sometimes the extra word is one which could come before or follow the word next to it but is not right in the context. In the sentences below one sentence in each pair has an extra word. Identify the extra word and decide why it is incorrect in the context.*

   1 a He has had plenty of opportunities and wasted them all.

      b He has had plenty of opportunities so I hope he makes the most of them.

   2 a People who are thought to be clever are promoted quickly.

      b People who thought to be clever are promoted quickly.

   3 a He doesn't fit in with the company image.

      b He doesn't fit in the company image.

   4 a If the power is important, then he's in the wrong job!

      b He likes the job for the power it gives him!

   5 a You can do a bigger and better than job.

      b You can do a bigger job, better than before.

3 *Often you have to read along the whole line or the whole sentence to understand that there is an extra word. Which part of the sentence tells you that the underlined words in the sentences below are extra?*

   1 <u>Although</u> we can't always achieve what we want and may need to limit our horizons.

   2 They do the same as those around them so, in this way, <u>that</u> they are successful.

   3 If you want to have some extra training, <u>so</u> you should speak to your manager.

   4 But, <u>because</u> to a certain extent that is how costs should be controlled: by managing the budget carefully.

Now check your answers to these questions and look back at your answers to Part Six of the Reading Test.

Writing

PART ONE

Question 1

- *The chart/graph below shows the quantity of coal bought by a company over a five-year period and the cost per ton. It also shows their purchases of other fuels and the cost per ton.*

- Using the information from the graph, write a short **report** comparing the cost of coal and other fuels and the amounts the company bought over the five-year period.

- Write **120–140** words.

Coal supplies

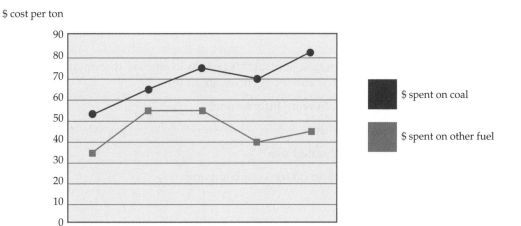

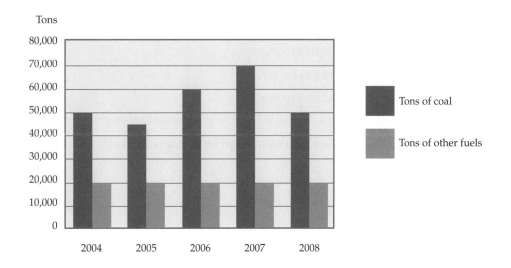

PART TWO

Questions 2–4

- Write an answer to one of the questions 2–4 in this part.
- Write **200–250** words.

Question 2

- Your company has recently sponsored a sporting event in order to gain publicity. Your manager has asked you to write a report on how successful this was.
- Write the **report** including the following information:
  - what kind of sponsorship your company gave
  - how successful the sponsorship was in terms of publicity generated
  - whether or not you would recommend sponsoring any more events.

Question 3

- Your department has just won a new contract and needs to employ more staff. Your manager has asked you to write a letter to recruitment agencies about this.
- Write the **letter** including the following information:
  - what the new contract involves
  - what skills the new staff should have
  - what you expect an agency to do for your company.

Question 4

- Your company car park is no longer big enough to provide parking for all the employees' cars. You decide to write a proposal to the Facilities department suggesting how the car parking situation can be improved.
- Write the **proposal** including the following information:
  - why the car parking problem has arisen
  - how you think the problem can be resolved
  - how your suggestion could be financed.

Before you write your answer to Part Two (letter), go on to pages 79–80.

Further Practice for Writing Part Two (letter)

EXAM INFORMATION

In Part Two of the Writing Test you may choose to write a piece of business correspondence. This is usually a letter that can be sent by email, fax or post. The letter is often to someone outside the company and may sometimes be a general or open letter to be sent to several recipients, e.g. a list of agencies or suppliers. The target reader may be someone you or the company has dealt with before (i.e. someone you know), or someone unknown.

A DETAILED STUDY

1 *It is important when you are writing a letter to think about your target reader. Look at question 3 on page 78. Who is the target reader?*

   a   a person in another company who you know

   b   an 'open' letter to unknown people in several companies

   c   a person in another company who you don't know

2 *The letter task will ask you to write a letter with a specific aim. Look at question 3 on page 78 again and decide what the purpose of the letter is.*

   a   to outline a problem and suggest a solution

   b   to apologise and offer an explanation

   c   to give information and make a request

   d   to make a complaint and ask for resolution

3 *Put these content points in order of how they should appear in your letter.*

   1   an explanation of the new contract

   2   closing statements

   3   an introduction to your company

   4   a description of what you require in any new staff

   5   a suggestion of what you want the reader to do

   6   your reason for writing

4 *You should always take 5 minutes to plan your writing as this will make sure you answer the question. Make notes on what you want to include in each paragraph.*

1	
2	
3	
4	
5	
6	

5 *Match the phrases (A–L) below with these content points (1–3).*

    1   what the new contract involves

    2   what skills the new staff should have

    3   what you expect an agency to do for your company.

    A   IT skills are essential

    B   This will require us to …

    C   … within a period of three weeks …

    D   It is to be completed by …

    E   We expect that we will need several …

    F   … conduct interviews …

    G   We have just negotiated ….

    H   … select the most appropriate …

    I   A knowledge of data processing would be useful …

    J   … agree terms with …

    K   This means we will have to …

    L   … experience of working with …

6 *Read the following extract of an answer a student wrote to Question 3 in Part Two. Then look at the marking criteria and decide how well the student has achieved each one by circling the relevant number.*

My name is Mr Smith and I work for XL Bricks. We've got a new contract to supply bricks to a company in the North but we don't have enough people to help. We need about ten extra staff if they can work for about three months until the contract is done. Ideally we need people who've done this kind of work before because we don't have time to train them.

Please let us know if you can help at all.

Many thanks

Criteria   1 = weak, 5 = very good

1	Content	1	2	3	4	5
2	Organisation	1	2	3	4	5
3	Range & accuracy	1	2	3	4	5
4	Register	1	2	3	4	5
5	Effect on target reader	1	2	3	4	5

Now write your own answer to Part Two of the Writing Test. Remember to check for spelling and grammar mistakes.

Listening

PART ONE

Questions 1–12

- You will hear Karen King, a Manager at Minehead Automotive, leading a session on team-building.

- As you listen, for questions **1–12**, complete the notes using up to **three** words or a number.

- You will hear the recording twice.

Successful teambuilding

Initial considerations

1 One of the first steps is to develop what Karen refers to as a .... of how the team should work.

2 Reaching agreement on a way forward requires practised .... skills.

3 Teams require members who will check the .... of a creative scheme for possible problems.

4 Members must be willing to help compensate for any .... that appears in the team's work.

5 Identify the full range of .... who will benefit from the team's work.

6 Remember to keep the team's '..' informed of progress.

How to keep members working as a team

7 You can encourage .... by organizing a number of joint events.

8 Sharing a meal regularly is an excellent scheme for reviewing team .... in a non-threatening way.

9 Work will go better if you develop an atmosphere of .... in the team.

Warning points

10 Prevent any .... between team members from becoming serious.

11 Make it clear to the team that .... is not an acceptable response.

12 Restrict any .... about members of the team as far as possible.

PART TWO

Questions 13–22

- You will hear five people talking about a presentation which they gave.
- For each extract there are two tasks. For Task One, decide why each person was worried about giving the presentation from the list **A–H**. For Task Two, decide what the outcome of the presentation has been for each speaker, from the list **A–H**.
- You will hear the recording twice.

TASK ONE – REASON FOR CONCERN

- For questions **13–17**, match the extracts with the reason given by the speaker, listed **A–H**.
- For each extract decide on the appropriate reason for concern before the presentation.
- Write **one** letter (**A–H**) next to the number of the extract.

13	**A** the length of the allocated slot
	B the clarity of the graphics
14	**C** the benefit of presenting at such an event
	D the physical limitations of the venue
15	**E** the balance of the session
	F the compatibility of the equipment
16	**G** the composition of the audience
17	**H** the availability of promotional materials

TASK TWO – OUTCOME

- For questions **18–22**, match the extracts with the outcome of the presentation, listed **A–H**.
- For each extract, choose the outcome each speaker describes.
- Write **one** letter (**A–H**) next to the number of the extract.

18	**A** The committee agreed to the proposal.
	B A potential supplier was identified.
19	**C** The company was asked to tender for a large development.
	D The event was included in the annual sales programme.
20	**E** The most recent models were featured in the national press.
21	**F** A training contract was agreed with a national leisure chain.
	G A participant asked to be sent more detailed information.
22	**H** A large organisation showed interest in one of the products.

PART THREE

Questions 23–30

- You will hear part of a radio interview with Clare Swinbrook, the manager of a manufacturing company, and James Kilbride, a professor of Business Administration, on the topic of communication.

- For each question **23–30**, mark **one** letter (**A, B** or **C**) for the correct answer.

- You will hear the recording twice.

23 What is Clare's attitude to today's communication channels?

    A   concern about the increasing insistence on the use of emails

    B   reluctance to give up discussing complex matters face to face

    C   irritation at the poor sound quality of voicemail messages

24 What do Clare and James agree is important in a meeting?

    A   listening carefully to the other people's views

    B   stating your own opinion as clearly as you can

    C   maintaining your company's position firmly

25 According to James, what is the main benefit of regular internal meetings?

    A   People can have an influence on company policy.

    B   It is an easy way for management to keep staff informed.

    C   Staff develop a sense of involvement with the company.

26 Clare refers to a 'communication code' to point out

    A   what unintended effects different forms of communication can have.

    B   how important it is to have a comprehensive induction programme.

    C   why colleagues should try to interact with new arrivals in their office.

27 What point is James making in his example of business language?

    A   Managers tend to talk too forcibly when addressing their staff.

    B   A careful choice of language can achieve improved results at work.

    C   Employees are likely to be alarmed when speaking to their superiors.

28 What is Clare's advice about talking to potential clients?

    A Make sure your speech is easy for them to follow.

    B Try to adopt the pace at which they talk.

    C Keep your eyes fixed on theirs.

29 James thinks that the most important point when writing is to

    A check everything for accuracy.

    B keep to the traditional rules.

    C write in a polite style.

30 Which of these does Clare see as influencing business communication most?

    A telephone communications

    B IT developments

    C air travel

Before you check your answers to Part Three, go on to page 85.

Further Practice for Listening Part Three

EXAM INFORMATION

In Part Three of the Listening Test, you hear a longer recording which may be a conversation, an interview or a discussion between two or more people. There are eight multiple choice questions with three options for each to choose from (A–C). The questions test your ability to understand the main points, attitudes and opinions expressed by interacting speakers. You will hear the recording twice.

A DETAILED STUDY

In the Reading Test, you can check the text as many times as you need in order to answer the questions. In the Listening Test, however, you will only hear the information twice so you need to focus on the key points. You may find it helpful to underline the important words in the options to help you do this. Remember that the information will not be expressed in the same way in the question as in the recording.

So, as in the other parts of the Listening Test, you need to listen for paraphrases.

Look at this example.

1   *What is Clare's attitude to today's communication channels?*
    A   concern about the increasing insistence on the use of emails
    B   reluctance to give up discussing complex matters face to face
    C   irritation at the poor sound quality of voicemail messages

Look at the beginning of the tapescript on p159.

    1   What does Clare actually say about emails?

    2   Is she concerned about the increasing use of emails?

    3   What does she say about face-to-face discussions?

    4   Is she reluctant to give up having face-to-face discussions?

    5   What does she say about voicemail messages?

    6   Is she irritated by the poor sound quality of voicemail messages?

Check the answers to these questions on p142.

2   *Now look at Question 24, underline key words and check the tapescript on p159.*

    1   Which of the options is mentioned by James?

    2   Which of the options is mentioned by Clare?

    3   How does Clare indicate that she shares James's view?

    4   What other ways do you know to indicate agreement and disagreement?

Agreement	Disagreement

Now check your answers to these questions and look at your answers to Part Three of the Listening Test.

Speaking

PART ONE

Conversation between the examiner and each candidate (about 3 minutes)

In Part One of the Speaking Test, the interlocutor asks questions to each of the candidates in turn. You have to give information about yourself and express personal opinions.

Here are some questions you may be asked:

1   Why did you choose to work in your area of business?

2   What aspect of your work do you think you are particularly good at?

3   What disadvantages are there to your present work situation?

4   Do you prefer to work alone or in a team?

5   How important is English in your work?

6   What would you most like to achieve in your working life?

7   How important is the manufacturing industry to your country?

8   How do you think working life is changing in your country?

9   What effect do you think IT developments will have on your country in future?

PART TWO

Mini-presentation (about 6 minutes)

In this part of the test, you are asked to give a short talk on a business-related topic. You have to choose one of the topics from the three below and then talk for about one minute. You have one minute to prepare your ideas.

A: Meetings: the factors involved in chairing meetings efficiently

B: Training: the importance of allowing junior staff to attend trade fairs

C: Corporate culture: the importance of keeping all staff informed about possible developments in an organisation

When you have given your presentation, your partner will ask you a question about what you have said. Here are some questions they may ask you:

Can you explain what you meant by…?

Could you go into a bit more detail about…?

A • How useful do you think it is it to follow an agenda?

 • Do you think it's important to try to keep to a time limit?

 • How can the chair prevent a participant from dominating the meeting?

B • What is the most important skill that staff can learn at a trade fair?

 • Do you think trade fairs are effective in marketing new products?

 • What effect do you think technology will have on the future of trade fairs?

C • Do you think there is some information which staff should not be told?

 • What is the best method of keeping everyone informed?

 • How far should each employee try to support the company in difficult times?

PART THREE

Discussion (about 7 minutes)

In this part of the test, you are given a discussion topic. You have 30 seconds to look at the prompt card and then about 3 minutes to discuss the topic with your partner. After that the examiner will ask you some more questions related to the topic.

For **two** candidates

Information Technology

The clothing company you work for is changing to a completely new computerised system which will control all aspects of the operation from purchasing to delivery. You have been asked to prepare a proposal for staff induction to the new system

Discuss and decide together:

- what methods should be adopted to ensure all staff are trained effectively

- what steps should be taken to prevent any initial problems from disrupting normal operations.

For **three** candidates

Information Technology

The clothing company you work for is changing to a completely new computerised system which will control all aspects of the operation from purchasing to delivery. You have been asked to prepare a proposal for staff induction to the new system

Discuss and decide together:

- what methods should be adopted to ensure all staff are trained effectively

- what steps should be taken to prevent any initial problems from disrupting normal operations

- how the introduction of the system might affect staff morale.

The examiner will then ask you some follow-up questions. Here are some questions you may be asked:

- What benefits do you think a company gains from a computerised operating system?

- How far should a company take into account the difficulty some people experience in adapting to new systems?

- Do you think that computerised systems are always the best way forward for a company?

- What do you think the long-term effects of computerisation will be on the job market?

Before you give your answer to Part Three, go on to page 89.

Further Practice for Speaking Part Three

EXAM INFORMATION

Part Three: The discussion

The third part of the speaking test starts with a discussion on a business-related topic between you and the other candidate(s). This lasts about three minutes. The interlocutor will then ask some questions to extend the discussion further. This part of the test is designed to check your ability to engage in the type of interaction that would be appropriate to a work environment. This will involve you in, for example, expressing and justifying your opinions, agreeing and disagreeing, speculating and comparing ideas.

A DETAILED STUDY

Strategies

The interlocutor will give you a topic with two or three discussion points. You have 30 seconds to read the topic and think about the discussion points. Try to collect some possible ideas to raise in the discussion.

During the discussion remember to:

- take an equal part in the interaction
- put forward ideas and support them
- listen to and comment on your partner's ideas
- reach decisions where possible
- speak as naturally as possible

Agreeing and disagreeing

Look at these different ways of agreeing and disagreeing and decide if they are

a – formal, or b – informal.

1. You're wrong.
2. That's a very good idea.
3. I'm not sure I agree with you there.
4. Absolutely!
5. I think that would be an excellent idea.
6. I think that might be rather a mistake.

Putting forward suggestions

Complete these sentences.

1. I think we .... introduce some face-to-face training.
2. What .... getting the team leaders to train their team members?
3. Why .... we ask the IT company to do the induction?
4. What .... we made a test about the system and everyone had to take it?
5. I think it .... be really good if we did a trial run of the system at the weekend.

Now check your answers to these questions and go back to Part Two of the Speaking Test.

BEC TEST 4

Reading

PART ONE

Questions 1–8

- Look at the statements below and at the five extracts from an article on the opposite page about a chain of department stores and supermarkets called John Lewis.

- Which extract (**A, B, C, D** or **E**) does each statement (**1–8**) refer to?

- For each statement (**1–8**), mark one letter (**A, B, C, D** or **E**) on your Answer Sheet.

- You will need to use some of these letters more than once.

- There is an example at the beginning, (**0**).

Example:

    0   It has a very low rate of staff turnover.

---

1   The company can survive an economic downturn because of the variety it provides.

2   The company partially belongs to the people who work for it.

3   The company has a better chance of survival than its competitors.

4   The company's profits are only healthy because of its website.

5   The company's customer service appears to be the cause of its success.

6   Staff are paid according to how well the company performs.

7   The company's performance is based on an increase in the number of people who are well off.

8   The company uses sites where it has a good target market.

A

Is it any different from other high street names?

Its radical philosophy comes from the company's messianic founder, John Spedan Lewis. His father had opened a shop in 1864. After rising rapidly through the family business, he wanted to create a company in which the employees had a greater stake. A system of committees, sub-committees and board positions were created to give workers a say. And crucially, they were given joint ownership of the company. That's why they reap a slice of the profits each year.

B

Does its approach work?

Judging by the results, it's hard not to reach the conclusion that motivated staff have a pretty big impact on a company's performance. Its staff retention rate is also very good, with 80 per cent staying for more than a year. And if you ask John Lewis customers, they are often fulsome in their praise of the staff. John Lewis (stores) and Waitrose (supermarkets) have come top in their respective categories in consumer surveys carried out for the last three years.

C

Are there any other factors in its success?

It is now a brand that consumers want to be associated with. The range offered by John Lewis protects it from falls in certain sectors. It also runs an extremely successful online arm. Waitrose, despite having just four per cent of the market, is arguably the only supermarket not to be losing market share to Tesco. Analysts say the reasons for that are clear: staff; quality products; and locating stores in pockets where they know they will find their customer base.

D

Is there any bad news for the store?

Sales in one week last month were down 3.4 per cent compared to the same week a year earlier. That made everyone sit up and take notice. It was just a sign that even a brand as mighty as John Lewis will have to contend with tricky market conditions this year. In fact, it could be the case that the company is best equipped to deal with falling consumer spending. The people who will still have disposable income burning a hole in their well-tailored pockets will be those in professional jobs. In other words, just the sort of people you might meet in John Lewis.

E

Is John Lewis really run differently from other companies?

It must be doing something differently, recording increased profits during a difficult period for retailers. Its success is more down to latching on to a growing upper-middle class customer base than any 'radical' philosophy. Many companies hand out bonuses. The shared ownership idea is just a gimmick. It succeeds not because of its philosophy, but owing to its very successful online operation.

PART TWO

Questions 9–14

- Read this text taken from an article about introducing a new management to a garden centre business.

- Choose the best sentence from the opposite page to fill each of the gaps.

- For each gap (**9–14**), mark one letter (**A–H**) on your Answer Sheet.

- Do not use any letter more than once.

- There is an example at the beginning, (**0**).

How a management technique designed for factories has taken root outdoors

The Horticultural Trades Association (HTA) says this year we will spend more than £5 billion on what is collectively known as the UK garden industry. Nowadays, of course, garden centres supply so much more than the traditional products, such as bedding plants, trees, shrubs and bulbs, which actually account for £2 billion worth of total sales. (**0**) ..H... Some centres have even won awards for their restaurants and shops rather than their horticultural skills. (**9**) .... Not quite, says the HTA's business development director Tim Briercliffe. Last week, during a visit to the Chessington Garden Centre, he was at pains to stress that while the tills are still ringing there has been a noticeable slowdown over the past couple of years. (**10**) ...... HTA members, who embrace garden centres, nurseries, landscapers and manufacturers, also face stiff competition in the traditional shrubs, trees and bulbs market from The Netherlands in particular. (**11**) ....

The trade association's answer is to introduce members to the concept of Lean management, a theory originally designed to improve efficiency on the Toyota car production line. (**12**) .... Essentially the Lean philosophy is that there are two basic tasks in any business function. (**13**) .... Where the customer is either better served or experiences fast and efficient service and wants the product as a result, is only added in a mere 5 per cent of actions in the supply chain. (**14**) .... The directors endorse the Lean principles as a means to run the business more efficiently. To date they estimate that 122 hours a week have been saved – equivalent to £45,000.

Example:

A By adopting such techniques for their own businesses, argues the HTA, garden centres will be better equipped to deal with the competition, as well as being more efficiently run operations in their own right.

B The first day is dedicated to theory, while the second is about mapping processes within the business and day three is for implementing an action plan.

C Having demonstrated that they can diversify into other, more lucrative, areas, you would think that all is rosy in the garden centre world.

D The argument is that 95 per cent of actions in most companies, such as delays, movement, excess production and searching for things, are non-value adding.

E Briercliffe points to the way in which Dutch growers have all co-operated to ensure that the whole process from planting to shop delivery is highly mechanised and that as a result they can offer the most competitive prices.

F In the case of Chessington Garden Centre, which started out growing budded roses and potatoes and selling eggs, this means it now makes an annual profit of more than £5m.

G Besides obvious rivals such as the Do-It-Yourself stores, supermarkets have declared plans to take a 'significant' share of the garden market in plants.

H The greater part of their income comes from the sale of manufactured goods. These cover anything from garden furniture, fountains and wooden decking to wind chimes, aquariums and patio heaters.

PART THREE

Questions 15–20

- Read the following extract from an article about how to sell, and the questions on the opposite page.

- For each question (**15–20**), mark one letter (**A, B, C** or **D**) on your Answer Sheet for the answer you choose.

Selling should be easy

1 Sales should essentially be easy. This is not to say that selling doesn't involve long hours, hard work, and sometimes unreasonable customers. But all sales training is based on replicating successful behaviour, things that worked for other people in the past. And whenever you get salespeople to describe their favourite and most successful sales, a very common theme is that
5 everything went smoothly and the process was essentially easy. Professional salespeople are also very aware that 'time is money' and the good ones learn how to manage the time they spend with each prospect, not wasting time on people who seem unable to make a decision.

Then you should think about vertical markets. You probably have products or services that are 'horizontal', such as IT support, office supplies or training courses which could theoretically be
10 sold to any type of customer. But if your first customer happens to be a dentist for example, start thinking about selling to other dentists. It's unlikely that your first sale was a fluke, to the only dentist in the world who needs what you do; more likely there are other dentists around with similar challenges.

You'll really hit the jackpot if your dentist first customer turns out to be a 'maven', an expert in
15 their particular field, but who also enjoys telling everyone they meet about the excellent new company they've discovered with great services, perfect for dentists. You should encourage them to spread the word in their local community of dentists, and particularly when they head off to a trade show or convention. However, you should be a bit wary of people who are only doing it for a financial upside; this is a dangerous road to go down for both parties; if people feel that
20 recommendations are being made purely for financial gain, they can become suspicious.

You will also begin to 'walk the walk and talk the talk' in the provision of your products and services to dentists. You will learn about their general problems, as well as those that are specific to what you do. It may be that Sunday afternoon is the only quiet time for dentists, so that's when you deliver your office supplies or arrange the back-up of their data. A good start is to find the
25 'tiniest thing' you can do for them. This is a good way to prove quickly what you do and also weed out any difficult customers, especially those that find it difficult to make quick buying decisions.

So will you be successful in ramping up your sales? It obviously depends on the quality of what you deliver, and the number of 'word of mouth' referrals you get. It's important to ask for
30 referrals and get everyone to tell their friends about what you do, but trying too hard can have the opposite effect; you can seem pushy and desperate. You want people to come to you because they want to, and the keys to success are simple: you need to be 'local', 'reliable' and 'nice'.

'Local' is all about geography, and you should focus your efforts as much as possible on people in your neighbourhood. Everyone likes to deal with someone who is 'just around the corner', not
35 just for ease of supply, but also swift resolution when things go wrong. 'Reliable' is only about making realistic promises on delivery and quality, and making sure you keep these promises, dealing with the occasional problems swiftly and fairly. And finally, 'nice' is about being easy to deal with, by always treating your customers how you wish to be treated yourself, even when it is sometimes not reciprocated.

15 The writer claims that selling should be easy because

   A normally it is a very straightforward process.

   B all you have to do is repeat certain actions.

   C it can be achieved in a limited amount of time.

   D it depends on getting people to make a decision.

16 The writer introduces the example of a dentist in the second paragraph

   A to illustrate the most profitable vertical market.

   B to explain how wide a customer base can be.

   C to show that sales are usually replicable.

   D to demonstrate the importance of a single sale.

17 What advice does the writer give in the third paragraph?

   A Ask certain customers to advertise for you.

   B Be careful about how you pay people.

   C Make sure you sell to experts first.

   D Refuse to pay people for recommendations.

18 Why does the writer recommend meeting customers on Sunday afternoons?

   A to demonstrate how hard you work

   B to show how you address customer needs

   C to find out how decisive the customer is

   D to increase sales in less busy times

19 In the fifth paragraph, the writer says you can try too hard because

   A the referrals you get may not result in sales.

   B you may not be able to rely on the quality of your products.

   C you don't need to tell all your friends about your business.

   D the effort you make will not increase your sales.

20 What point is the writer making in the last paragraph?

   A Your best sales will come from people in your local area.

   B Being reliable is the least important of the three qualities mentioned.

   C Success is only possible if customers enjoy doing business with you.

   D It is vital to have a consistent approach if you want successful sales.

Before you check your answers to Parts One to Three, go on to pages 96–97.

Further Practice for Reading Parts One, Two and Three

USING READING TEXTS TO EXPAND YOUR VOCABULARY

1   *Expand your vocabulary by checking the meaning of any business phrases or expressions in the reading texts which are unfamiliar. Use the context in which they appear to help you understand meaning.*

Match items 1–8 to their meaning a–h. Try to do this without using your dictionary; use the texts to help you.

1   to have a stake in something (Part 1 A)

2   to reap a slice of something (Part 1 A)

3   to sit up and take notice (Part 1 D)

4   to latch onto something (Part 1 E)

5   to think all is rosy (Part 2 C)

6   to hit the jackpot (Part 3 para 3)

7   to ramp up sales (Part 3 para 5)

8   to spread the word (Part 3 para 3)

a   to attach yourself to something

b   to tell a lot of people about something

c   to assume that everything is going well

d   to have an investment or financial interest in a company

e   to make a lot of money or be successful

f   to increase your business dramatically

g   to get something, especially something good, as a result of what you have done

h   to become alert or aware that something is going on

2   *Business vocabulary contains a lot of compound nouns and strong collocations. Use the reading texts to expand your knowledge of these.*

Match the words on the left (1–10) to the words on the right (a–j) to create compound nouns or typical collocations. Use the texts to help you if necessary.

1	joint (Part 1)	a	markets
2	staff (Part 1)	b	goods
3	market (Part 1)	c	income
4	customer (Part 1)	d	retention
5	disposable (Part 1)	e	gain
6	stiff (Part 2)	f	share
7	manufactured (Part 2)	g	ownership
8	vertical (Part 3)	h	supplies
9	office (Part 3)	i	competition
10	financial (3)	j	base

EXAM TIPS FOR THE READING TEST

3   *In the Reading Test you have one hour to read and answer questions on six parts. Some texts are longer than others, i.e. Parts One, Two and Three, so you will need to allow more time for these.*

     Complete the chart with the amount of time you think you should allow for each part of the reading test.

Part 1	Part 2	Part 3	Part 4	Part 5	Part 6

Next time you do a test, or if you repeat any of the tests in this book, try to do the reading test within the times listed in the answer section.

4   *Which is the best way to do parts 1, 2 and 3 in the Reading Test? Why?*

     1   Read the questions very carefully, then look at the texts.

     2   Skim the text, then look at the questions and locate the answers.

     3   Read the text very carefully, then look at the questions and then check both together.

5   *What should you do if you don't know or can't find the answer to a question?*

     1   Keep looking for the answer before you move on to the next question.

     2   Ignore it and lose the mark – it is more important to finish the test.

     3   Leave it and move on. Then go back in any remaining time to see if you can find the answer. If you can't, then guess the answer.

     4   Leave it and move on. Then go back in any remaining time to see if you can find the answer. If you can't, leave it blank.

Now check your answers to these questions and look back at your answers to Parts One, Two and Three of the Reading Test.

PART FOUR

Questions 21–30

- Read the article below about niche businesses.
- Choose the correct word to fill each gap from **A, B, C** or **D** on the opposite page.
- For each question **21–30**, mark one letter (**A, B, C** or **D**) on your Answer Sheet.
- There is an example at the beginning, (**0**).

The best business ideas

There are countless examples of small businesses started by people working in particular industries who spot (**0**) ……….. that their current employers either do not see or fill inadequately. Such enterprises can sometimes grow to a size to (**21**) ………. the original businesses from which they spring.

Just as with management (**22**) ………., where formerly languishing companies suddenly power ahead, many niche businesses thrive on the back of the specialist knowledge gained by their founders while working in the original companies. In some cases, they are able to transform an activity that was once an (**23**) ………. or at least a nuisance into a profitable entity in its own right.

This is especially common in industries such as oil and steel, where the (**24**) ………. activity of finding and selling oil or making steel is surrounded by (**25**) …………. activities that are not central to the main purpose of the business but are nevertheless crucial to its success, because if done efficiently they can dramatically (**26**) ………. its finances. It is no coincidence that some of the early examples of (**27**) ………. such functions as finance and facilities management were seen in the oil industry.

Robert Leigh, founder of the property company Devono, took a different approach. Rather than setting himself up as (**28**) ………. a service to his former employers, he is using his knowledge of the property industry to compete with them directly in a particular (**29**) ………. of the market.

Devono was set up to represent tenants in property (**30**) ………... .The company may not win as much repeat business as those representing landlords, but Leigh claims that last year it moved more businesses than any other property company in London.

Example:

       A gaps   **B** spaces   **C** holes   **D** blanks

	A	B	C	D
0	▬	☐	☐	☐

21   **A**   pressure   **B**   compare   **C**   compete   **D**   rival

22   **A**   purchases   **B**   mergers   **C**   buyouts   **D**   takeovers

23   **A**   overhead   **B**   outflow   **C**   outcome   **D**   overload

24   **A**   critical   **B**   core   **C**   chief   **D**   essential

25   **A**   substitute   **B**   extra   **C**   ancillary   **D**   accessory

26   **A**   intensify   **B**   heighten   **C**   reinforce   **D**   enhance

27   **A**   outputting   **B**   offloading   **C**   outsourcing   **D**   offsetting

28   **A**   creating   **B**   tendering   **C**   producing   **D**   providing

29   **A**   segment   **B**   sector   **C**   portion   **D**   department

30   **A**   transactions   **B**   trades   **C**   promotions   **D**   undertakings

PART FIVE

Questions 31–40

- Read the article below about meetings.
- For each question **31–40** write one word in CAPITAL LETTERS on your Answer Sheet.
- There is an example at the beginning, **(0)**.

Example: **0** A G O □ □ □ □ □

'Sorry, I can't take your call right now. I'm in a meeting ... again!'

Most people in business have a strong sense that meetings are demanding more and more of their time. Fifty years **(0)** .... meetings were barely necessary – the boss decided what was going to happen and told employees.

Now everything in business is discussed extensively in large meetings attended **(31)** .... anybody who has the remotest interest in the subject. Larger and more complex organisations have more meetings than smaller companies, even adjusting for **(32)** ....greater size. Senior managers now seem to do little else than rush **(33)** .... one discussion to another.

Increases in global trade and in corporate mergers are tending to increase the need for long-distance travel to meetings. **(34)** .... a consequence, corporate travel is a growing part of carbon emissions. It would be easy to say we must reverse the trend **(35)** .... more meetings. Unfortunately, it is not going to be easy. Some interesting recent research shows that most of the attendees at corporate meetings do complain about the waste of time involved, but when questioned in private, the picture changes. **(36)** .... most attendees saw room for improvement, meetings were seen as valuable in helping build plans for action and in making employees feel **(37)** .... of the organisation.

The researchers comment that meetings play a large role in employee socialisation, relationship building **(38)** .... also shaping of the corporate culture. The unpalatable fact is that huge organisations contain **(39)** .... complexity and ambiguity that the rising number of meetings plays a vital role in giving employees some sense of their employer's objectives and tactics. People in large, amorphous organisations may find it difficult to do **(40)** .... the reassurance and information gained by frequent contact with colleagues.

PART SIX

Questions 41–52

- Read the text below about the construction industry.

- In most of the lines **41–52** there is one extra word. It is either grammatically incorrect or does not fit in with the meaning of the text. Some lines, however, are correct.

- If a line is correct, write **CORRECT** on your Answer Sheet.

- If there is an extra word in the line, write **the extra word** in CAPITALS on your Answer Sheet.

- The exercise begins with two examples (**0**) and (**00**).

Examples:

| **0** | C | O | R | R | E | C | T | |
| **00** | A | N | D | | | | | |

Careers in the construction industry

  0   More than £50 bn a year is spent on construction, making it the largest

00   single and manufacturing industry in the UK. The variety of qualified

41   careers available would satisfy the most ambitious school leaver or

42   undergraduate. So why, as according to the Construction Industry

43   Training Board (CITB), are 70 per cent of construction companies which

44   based in the South-East concerned by recruitment problems? In fact

45   there is a skills shortage that threatens to stifle the industry's growth, a

46   greater threat indeed than any more perceived economic recession.

47   Many firms are now working at full capacity and are most unable to bid

48   for new work as they either lack the staff to service the contracts.

49   Although there is a negative image of the construction industry that

50   focuses entirely on construction sites (rather than the much overlooked

51   professional side) and it is fuelled by stereotypical adverts and the TV

52   programmes. Managerial careers in construction are varied, by making

      full use of people's creative, technical and business skills.

Further practice for Reading Parts Four, Five and Six

EXAM INFORMATION

Tips

Here are some tips to help you complete Parts Four to Six of the Reading Test.

- Make sure you read the instructions and the title of the passage carefully. This can help you to focus in quickly on the topic of the text.

- It is important to read through the whole text before you start trying to answer the questions. Again this will give you an idea of the scope of the text and it will also allow your subconscious to start working on the possible answers.

- In Part Four, check each option carefully and try it out in the space. It sometimes helps to say the sentence silently to see if it sounds right. Do not home straight in on one option.

- In Part Five, work out what type of word (noun, verb, adjective etc.) is required in the space. Then think of possible answers. Don't forget to check whether a noun should be singular or plural, or whether a verb should be present or past, by looking carefully at the surrounding text.

- In Part Six, remember to look beyond the particular line to the rest of the sentence. When you think you have identified an extra word, try saying the sentence silently to see if it makes sense and sounds right.

- Remember to read through the whole passage at the end, inserting the answers you have chosen. This may help you to spot if one of your selections is not right.

PREPARATION STRATEGIES

Look at the different preparation strategies and decide which Part (Four, Five or Six) each strategy would benefit most.

1   Find out what common mistakes in grammar or vocabulary you make most often, by looking through past exercises and homework or asking your teacher. Write down sentences using the correct versions and learn them by heart.

2   Read as many short newspaper articles about business topics as possible and note down any useful words and phrases.

3   Check a classmate's first draft of a piece of business writing and suggest appropriate amendments.

4   Think of a common business topic, for example, recruitment, and write down as many words as you can think of connected to the topic. Look some of them up in a Business English dictionary and check the prepositions that go with them, for example, *apply for a job, fill in an application form.*

PART ONE

Question 1

- The chart below shows sales of different types of holiday in 2008 in a travel company.

- Using the information from the chart, write a short **report** comparing the sales of different types of holiday.

- Write **120–140** words.

Sales of holidays 2008

Sales in 000,000

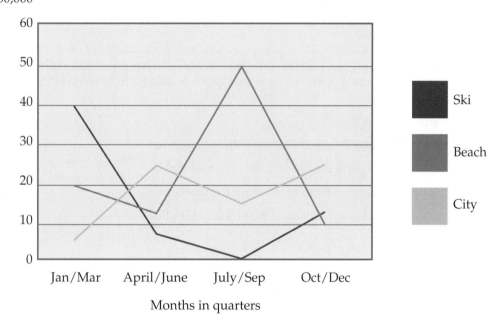

Months in quarters

PART TWO

Questions 2–4

- Write an answer to **one** of the questions 2–4 in this part.
- Write **200–250** words.

Question 2

- Your company has just completed a marketing campaign for some of its products or services. Your line manager has asked you to write a report on the success of this campaign.
- Write the **report** including the following information:
  - what marketing strategies were used in the campaign
  - how successful the campaign was
  - what improvements could be made.

Question 3

- A supplier to your company has just raised their costs and you have also had problems with their service. This is the third rise in a row so your manager has asked you to write to the company about this problem.
- Write the **letter** to the supplier:
  - describing what problems you have had with their service
  - explaining why you think the rise in costs is unreasonable
  - outlining what you expect them to do about the problem
  - saying what your company will do if the problem is not resolved.

Question 4

- Your company currently uses an external supplier to deliver training but your department has not been very satisfied with this training. You decide to write a proposal to the Head of the Training Department suggesting that in-house training may be more effective.
- Write the **proposal** including the following information:
  - why you are dissatisfied with the external training service
  - why you think in-house training would be more successful
  - how an in-house training programme could be set up.

Before you write your answer to Part Two (proposal), go on to pages 105–106.

Further practice for Writing Part Two (proposal)

EXAM INFORMATION

In Part Two of the Writing Test you may choose to write a proposal. Like a report, this should be clearly organised and use headings. It should also have an introduction and conclusion. You will be told what points to include in the task but can draw on your own experience of the world of work in order to relate it to something you are familiar with. You should always plan your answer carefully to make sure you address all the content points, as covering these is part of assessment.

A DETAILED STUDY

1　*Who is a proposal written for?*

    1　somebody you don't know external to the company

    2　a boss or line manager

    3　a member of staff who works for you

    4　a colleague at the same level as you in the company

2　*Decide which of these features are true for a report and which for a proposal. Some of them apply to both.*

1	headings	6	language of suggestion
2	formal or objective language	7	a focus on a future activity
3	language of evaluation	8	an analysis of a current situation
4	an introduction and conclusion	9	language of persuasion
5	a focus on past activity		

3　*A proposal is normally written in order to persuade someone to accept an idea or suggestion. You need to use persuasive strategies for your proposal to be effective.*

A　Language	B　Content
• use emphasis: *It is absolutely vital that ...* *It is extremely important for the company to ...* *Staff were totally convinced of the effectiveness of ....* • use persuasive verbs and structures: *I would urge you to consider ...* *It is essential/critical that ...* *There is an urgent need for ...*	• give reasons to support your argument • give examples of how your suggestion(s) could work *Look at the proposal on page 104. Make a list of:* 1　the reasons why the external training service should be dropped 2　the reason why an in-house service would be more successful, with examples of predicted results and/or benefits 3　an example of how an in-house programme could work *Check your ideas against the sample answer on page 147.*

4   *Choose the best section headings from each pair below for the proposal on page 104.*

   1   **a**   Purpose

      b   About this proposal

   2   **a**   Reasons I am dissatisfied with the external training service

      b   Problems with the external training service

   3   **a**   Why I think in-house training would be better

      b   The advantages of in-house training

   4   **a**   How an in-house training programme could be organised

      b   The ways we could have an in-house training programme

   5   **a**   Conclusion

      b   Recommendation

5   *Proposals (and reports) use the passive tense a lot in order to show an objective stance.*

   Rewrite the underlined words in each sentence to make the sentence more formal. You may have to change   verbs into the passive and make other changes to the sentence.

   1   The feedback <u>which we got</u> from staff indicated <u>they were not happy</u> with the training.

   ....

   2   <u>I interviewed</u> all the staff in the department and <u>they complained</u> about the programme.

   ....

   3   <u>We could use</u> staff in the IT department to train others in IT systems.

   ....

   4   The Head of HR <u>suggested running</u> training sessions during the lunch hours.

   ....

   5   <u>I think we</u> should <u>look into</u> employing trainers in the company.

   ....

6   *Paragraphing and punctuation are important if you want your business correspondence to create a good impression. Add punctuation and paragraphing to the following:*

the problem with the external training service is that its trainers are not as good as they could be although some of them have considerable experience others do not they also tend to run generic courses which are not specifically tailored to our needs we need some generic training such as health and safety basic IT skills etc but we also need some specifically targeted training which could probably best be delivered by people who work in house and know the company well my suggestion is that we identify people within the company who have specific skills that they can usefully pass on we could then give them some help in how to run training sessions

Now write your own answer to Part Two of the Writing Test. Remember to check for spelling and grammar mistakes.

Listening

PART ONE

Questions 1–12

- You will hear George Crump, Head of the Health and Safety team at Martins Finance, giving a talk about stress management in his company.

- As you listen, for questions **1–12**, complete the notes using up to **three** words or a number.

- You will hear the recording twice.

Stress management at Martins Finance

Starting point

1 The problem was detected when .... were routinely checked.

Fact finding phase

2 Written information was provided by existing staff, and Personnel also conducted .... with the relevant people.

3 Informal feedback was sought from managers, ... and employees.

4 George Crump chaired the .... , formed to evaluate the information.

5 It became clear that facilities like the .... were not well known.

6 A .... was devised to indicate what steps should be taken.

Key features of managers' training programme

7 First, they were told that all staff had a .... for stress management.

8 They were given a '...' to help them recognise likely stress points.

9 They were taught to select the right, so-called .... to cope with stress.

10 Most people felt the focus on the .... of stress was worthwhile.

11 Discussing .... enabled participants to see how they could help staff.

Outcome

12 The money wasted on stress-related time off fell by a total of ....

PART TWO

Questions 13–22

• You will hear five people talking about customer relations.

• For each extract there are two tasks. For Task One, decide which customer relations strategy each person adopted from the list **A–H**. For Task Two, decide what each speaker says has been the main benefit of a focus on customer relations, from the list **A–H**.

• You will hear the recording twice.

TASK ONE – STRATEGY ADOPTED

• For questions **13–17**, match the extracts with the customer relations strategy, listed **A–H**.

• For each extract choose the customer relations strategy adopted by each person.

• Write one letter (**A–H**) next to the number of the extract.

13 ....

14 ....

15 ....

16 ....

17 ....

A   Ensure all customer documentation is clear.

B   Provide a helpful after-sales service.

C   Make sure staff are well informed about the products.

D   Offer customers that little bit extra.

E   Ensure staff behaviour does not give offence.

F   Try to explain any problems clearly.

G   Provide easy-to-use feedback forms.

H   Try to see the company from the customer's position.

TASK TWO – MAIN BENEFIT

• For questions **18–22**, match the extracts with the main benefit that has been gained by a focus on customer relations, listed **A–H**.

• For each extract, choose the main benefit each speaker describes.

• Write one letter (**A–H**) next to the number of the extract.

18 ....

19 ....

20 ....

21 ....

22 ....

A   increased staff satisfaction

B   reduced marketing costs

C   higher profit margins

D   increased customer retention rates

E   a stronger position in the market place

F   more accessible systems

G   a more flexible organisation

H   products that meet market needs better

PART THREE

Questions 23–30

- You will hear two managers called Mark and Pam, who are attending the same conference, discussing the problems of staff retention.

- For each question **23–30**, mark one letter (**A, B** or **C**) for the correct answer.

- You will hear the recording twice.

23 In Mark's view, what part does money play in retaining staff?

    A It lessens in importance as people achieve more senior posts.

    B It becomes more attractive when living costs increase.

    C It has to be accompanied by valuable benefits.

24 Which non-material advantage does Pam think might help to keep staff?

    A pleasant colleagues

    B a sense of community

    C a comfortable office

25 Mark refers to someone who has worked with him for years to suggest that

    A public awards are a good way to motivate staff.

    B workmates need to show they value each other's work.

    C big prizes serve to make people much more competitive.

26 What do Pam and Mark both think about managers today?

    A They are so overworked that they can't oversee their team properly.

    B Training has made them more aware of their support role.

    C An unhelpful attitude often leads to staff resignations.

27 Mark thinks that the flexibility most people would value is being able to

    A organise their work time round the family.

    B take a period of time off unpaid to go travelling.

    C transfer their work entirely to their home.

28 In Pam's view, how would staff feel about being asked to do more training?

    A They would only consider it if the company paid the fees.

    B They could object to having to give up some of their free time.

    C They might welcome it if it helped to develop their career path.

29 According to Mark, what should concern a company if staff keep jobs for some time?

    A Boredom may make them careless in the way they work.

    B They may need extra challenges to maintain their commitment.

    C They may become too well-established and prove hard to dismiss.

30 What solution does Pam suggest to the problem of blocked promotion?

    A Offer short fixed-term contracts to some senior staff.

    B Introduce a system in which some managerial posts rotate.

    C Second some staff to other companies on a temporary basis.

Further practice for Listening Parts One, Two and Three

EXAM INFORMATION

Look at this list of exam tips and decide which part of the Listening Test each tip refers to.

1 Decide whether to attempt both tasks during the first listening.

2 Check that you have spelt the answers correctly.

3 Write clearly using capital letters.

4 Underline key words in the three options.

5 Read the instructions above the task very carefully.

6 If you are not absolutely sure of the answer, guess.

A DETAILED STUDY

Part One

Answers that are written incorrectly will not be awarded a mark. It is therefore very important to check that you know how to spell common business words.

Look at these sentences. There is a mistake in each one. Identify the mistake and correct it.

1 The personal department keeps records of absences through sickness.

2 I think the principal function of a Line Manager is to supervise their team.

3 You'll find the printer cartridges in the stationary cupboard.

4 The company nearly went bankrumpt last year.

5 The core competencys are all explained in the staff manual.

6 His secreatarial skills are definitely above average.

7 We need to find sufficient accomodation for our conference delegates.

8 It's time to prepare for the annual staff apraisals.

9 Journalists have to take care not to infringe the copywrite laws.

10 Inefficency creates a lot of unnecessary expense.

Part Two

Check what the focus of each task is before you listen and note the verb tense which is used. Look at the instructions for Part Two now on page 108.

1 What is the focus for Task One?

2 Is this task focused on a past, present or future action?

3 What is the focus for Task Two?

4 Is this task focused on the past, present or future?

5 What are the two key words in this task?

Now look at the tapescript below and follow the instructions.

6   Underline the two sentences that provide the answer to Task One.

7   Select the correct option from the Task One list.

8   Circle the distractors for Task One.

9   Put a line through the phrase that rules out those distractors.

10   Underline the answer for Task Two.

11   Circle the distractor for Task Two.

12   Put a line through the phrase that rules out that distractor.

We trade in a competitive area, so we decided to try to give our company a bit of an edge by focusing on customer relations. We brainstormed some options and then analysed how viable they were. Some important items like the brochures and customer response questionnaires had recently been revised so those were put on one side. Someone suggested that sales staff could be encouraged to imagine how they'd feel if they were purchasing goods from us – how they'd prefer to be treated. We decided to try that and it made a difference. After six months it was clear that the balance sheet looked much healthier. We also expect our advertising budget next year to be lower than in previous years, but time will tell on that one.

Now try a similar procedure with another of the Part Two tapescripts on page 161.

Part Three

Here are a few suggestions on how to maximize your chances in this task.

*   Use the 45-second preparation time well. Read through each question and underline what you think are the key words. Try to get a sense of where the interview or discussion will be heading.

*   While you are listening to the recording for the first time, make a preliminary decision on the three options for each question. Put a cross against any option which you think is impossible. Put a question mark against any option(s) that you think are possible. Only put a tick against an option if you are 100 per cent sure that it is the correct answer.

*   While you are listening to the recording for the second time, focus on the options that you have put question marks next to. This will allow you to firm up your decision. Listen for paraphrases of the terms in the options. Check whether the speaker is stressing the point or discounting it with negative terms like 'though'.

*   If you really can't decide between two options, guess. It is better than leaving a blank on the answer sheet.

Now check your answers to the Part One and Part Two exercises and then look back at your answers to the three Listening Test tasks on pages 107–109.

Speaking

PART ONE

Conversation between the examiner and each candidate (about 3 minutes)

In Part One of the Speaking Test, the interlocutor asks questions to each of the candidates in turn. You have to give information about yourself and express personal opinions.

Here are some questions you may be asked:

1   Why did you decide to take your current job?

2   What aspect of your job would you most like to change?

3   How far did your school / college prepare you for working life?

4   What further training would you like to undertake?

5   Would you like to run your own business?

6   What qualities do you think a Managing Director needs?

7   How important are business qualifications in finding a good job in your country?

8   What effect is the internet having on retail outlets in your country?

9   How do you think work patterns are changing in your country?

PART TWO

Mini-presentation (about 6 minutes)

In this part of the test, you are asked to give a short talk on a business-related topic. You have to choose one of the topics from the three below and then talk for about one minute. You have one minute to prepare your ideas.

> **A: Staffing:** the factors involved in attempting to retain trained staff

> **B: Health and safety:** how to ensure that all employees are following health and safety guidelines

> **C: Corporate culture:** the importance to an organisation of encouraging a spirit of innovation

When you have given your presentation, your partner will ask you a question about what you have said. Here are some questions they may ask you:

Can you explain what you meant by...?

Could you go into a bit more detail about...?

A • What are the disadvantages to a company of a high staff turnover?

 • How important is salary in keeping staff?

 • Why do you think people decide to leave a company after a short time?

B • What incentives can a company offer to staff who follow the guidelines?

 • Would you impose fines on staff who ignore one of the guidelines?

 • Do you think all health and safety guidelines are necessary?

C • Can innovation be taught or is it a natural talent?

 • How can a company reward staff who come up with innovative ideas?

 • Do you think continual innovation is always positive?

PART THREE

Discussion (about 7 minutes)

In this part of the test, you are given a discussion topic. You have 30 seconds to look at the prompt card and then about 3 minutes to discuss the topic with your partner. After that the examiner will ask you some more questions related to the topic.

For **two** candidates

Exhibition stand

The clothing company you work for is thinking of exhibiting at a large international trade fair for the first time. It has reserved a small stand, but it hopes to display the company's expertise to the full. You have been asked to make some recommendations.

Discuss and decide together:

- how to make the most of a limited space
- what might be done to attract a range of visitors to the stand.

For **three** candidates

Exhibition stand

The clothing company you work for is thinking of exhibiting at a large international trade fair for the first time. It has reserved a small stand, but it hopes to display the company's expertise to the full. You have been asked to make some recommendations.

Discuss and decide together:

- how to make the most of a limited space
- what might be done to attract a range of visitors to the stand
- how to select the team to make the final design for the stand.

The examiner will then ask you some follow-up questions. Here are some questions you may be asked:

- What benefits do you think employees gain from working together on a project?
- How important is it for companies to be represented at trade fairs?
- What should a company consider when it is trying to project a new image?
- How far do you think international trade fairs can help a company to grow?

Further practice for Speaking Parts One, Two and Three

EXAM TIPS

Part One

- Don't give minimal answers. Add a reason or state a preference, even if it is just a yes/no question.

- Try to vary the grammatical structures and vocabulary that you use.

Complete these responses.

1   What further training would you like to undertake?

   I'd like to do some courses in ....

2   Would you like to run your own business?

   Yes, I would ....

3   How do you think work patterns are changing in your country?

   I think people are working longer hours ....

Part Two

- Time yourself when you practise giving a mini-presentation. It is important to get used to speaking for a minute.

- Use a range of discourse markers to help you structure your mini-presentation.

Complete these sentences using an appropriate word or phrase from the box.

a The main problem   b On the other hand   c In my opinion   d One important area   e Finally

1   Regular meetings are useful to help a team bond; .... you don't want them to take up too much time.

2   .... I'd like to conclude by emphasising the need for a clear career path.

3   .... is staff training. This helps to keep people up-to-date with technology.

4   .... the best way to keep staff happy is to praise their work.

5   .... for long-staying staff is that they become bored with their routine tasks.

- Listen carefully while your partner is giving his or her mini-presentation. As you listen, note down a couple of questions to ask at the end.

Look at Topic A again on page 114 and think of two questions to ask:

6   How important..(work environment)?

7   What role..(money)?

Part Three

- The interlocutor will ask you some questions to extend the discussion. Listen carefully to the questions and give a well-structured answer. Try not to repeat ideas or language that you have already used in the discussion.

Match a question in List A with the beginning of an answer in List B. Then complete the answers.

List A

1   Are trade fairs worth all the trouble and expense?

2   What is the key point for staff on a stand to remember?

3   What is the purpose of handing out merchandise?

4   Is it important for senior staff to attend trade fairs?

List B

a)   It can act as a reminder ......

b)   They can learn what ......

c)   Some definitely are so ......

d)   Their role is to ......

Key and Explanation

TEST 1

p8–9 READING Part One

Questions 1–8

0 **B:** *Alternatively, you could join a strategy consultancy.*

1 **D:** *You need … inevitably reprioritise in accordance with the client's needs.*

2 **D:** *… to recognize the importance of every member of the team.*

3 **B:** *… many … grew out of audit firms …*

4 **E:** *Consultants have to be astute enough … hinder the progress of a project …*

5 **A:** *But fear not* (referring back to the fact that you may not have management experience).

6 **A:** *New entrants will … under the guidance of an experienced consultant.*

7 **C:** *… it's like being able to both diagnose a health problem and do the surgery.*

8 **E:** *You have to tell it how it is* and *You need that strong spine.*

Further practice and guidance (p10–11)

A detailed study

1

1 **C:** *… it doesn't exactly sound exciting … But in fact … resolving the problem.*

2 **E:** *Consultants have to be astute enough* and *You have to tell it how it is.*

3 **A:** *A good proportion of people entering consultancy do so after several years of industry experience. … But fear not – if you are a team player with sharp intellect, ambition and good communication skills, consultancy firms may be willing to train you up themselves.*

4 **B:** *You could opt for a generalist consulting firm, which offers a wide range of services from strategy consulting and human resources to IT and, in some cases, outsourcing on a global basis. Alternatively, you could join a strategy consultancy. … they primarily offer strategic advice to companies.*

5 **D:** *You need to be able to prioritise and then inevitably reprioritise in accordance with the client's needs … should also be capable of seeing a whole picture from fragments of information, able to determine the key to moving to the next step and have a very clear appreciation of the law of unforeseen consequences. … also need to be a team player with the ambition to be captain and the humility to recognise the importance of every member of the team.*

2 **1** outcomes

A: you'll develop skills and experience and gain ever more responsibility

C: articulate the issue they are grappling with and resolving the problem

E: This is all part and parcel of providing consultancy

2 attitudes and/or behaviour

A: (sharp intellect), ambition

D: appreciation of the law of unseen consequences, ambition, humility

E: astute, strong spine

3 skills

A: good communication skills

C: writing reports, listening to clients, resolving the problem

D: prioritise, reprioritise, seeing a whole picture, team player

E: have a strategy

3 **0** Consultants may <u>be able</u> to work for a <u>specialist firm</u>.

1 Consultants must be prepared to <u>change</u> the way they have <u>evaluated a project</u>.

2 Consultants <u>need</u> to <u>value</u> the <u>colleagues</u> they work with.

3 <u>Large</u> consultancies often have a <u>background</u> in <u>accounting</u>.

4   Consultants <u>need</u> to be able to <u>assess</u> each person's <u>contribution</u> <u>accurately</u>.

5   You <u>can become</u> a consultant even if you have <u>no management experience</u>.

6   <u>Mentoring</u> is often used to help <u>trainees</u> become <u>more effective</u> at the job.

7   Consultancy work is <u>satisfying</u> because you see the <u>end result</u> of a project.

8   Consultants <u>must not be frightened</u> of being <u>honest</u>.

4   0   an expert in

1   alter, reprioritise, transform, diversify

2   recognise the importance of

3   audit, finance

4   be able to spot, diagnose, evaluate, estimate

5   not, none etc.

6   working with, under the guidance of

7   outcome, resolution, consequences

8   being frank, telling it how it is

p12–13 READING Part Two

Questions 9–14

0   **H:** *My experience is that you can't.*

The clause after **can't** is not there but is a response to the question *How can I show them … ?*

9   **D:** *All the talking in the world about changing the way people work will not carry any weight compared with **managers and employees discovering the gap** themselves.*

This means that … which follows this gap refers to managers and employees discovering the gap themselves.

10   **B:** *This is important; they need to look at more than just the **financial aspects**.*

This refers to discussing the goal in the previous sentence. *The numbers* in the sentence after the gap refers to financial aspects.

11   **G:** *Different managers have different perspectives and it is always good to see if there is a consensus in how the challenge is seen.*

Different managers refers to *more than one group* in the previous sentence.

12   **A:** *Rest assured, **there will be a gap** and, in some organisations, the gap is rather intimidating.*

there will be a gap refers to *compare* in the previous sentence. *But* in the sentence after the gap refers to the intimidating gap.

13   **F:** *Then ask them what they are prepared to do differently, beginning tomorrow, to close the gaps.*

Then refers back to the fact that some activity or action has taken place before. *Them* refers to the managers in the previous sentence.

14   **C:** *But managers need to realise that the organisation is the way it is because of past decisions and **the way they acted** on them.*

But refers back to the problem in the previous sentence (rejection, etc). *if they do things differently* in the sentence after the gap refers back to **the way they acted**.

Choice E: *This is lame, old thinking that is not sustainable nor workable.*

There is no place in the text where this sentence would fit.

p14–15 READING Part Three

Questions 15–20

15   **C:** *launching new products or repositioning faded brands is increasingly the subject of scientific scrutiny* (line 8) and *Global brands want to make sure their products succeed across national boundaries* (line 14).

A: The text implies detailed research reduces risk, not that it ensures success.

B: The text says that products are available worldwide, but not that they have to be.

D: The text says that *innovation is the norm* (line 6) but not that consumers will stop buying brands that don't innovate regularly.

16   **D:** *filming … in order to … uncover hidden truths* (line 37).

A: This is what happens but it is not mentioned as an advantage.

B: The participants are aware they are being filmed though do become relaxed about it – *the novelty of being filmed will wear off* (line 43).

C: Although there are *Hours and hours of video* (line 49) the text does not mention whether or not it is easy to gather.

17 A: *Film has the advantage over questionnaires because the camera doesn't lie.* (line 63)

B: The text doesn't mention if participants have to complete paperwork or not.

C: The text mentions the number of households or individuals who are usually filmed but doesn't say this is an advantage.

D: The text says that data is collected over two or three days but doesn't say this is an advantage.

18 B: *While supermarkets mine data from micro-chipped loyalty cards to segment markets and target special offers, this kind of number-crunching misses the bigger picture* (line 87)

A: The text does not mention whether the data is predictable or not.

C: The text does not say whether or not they allow for human interpretation of data.

D: The text says they are limited but does not mention whether or not they need improving.

19 D: *Sometimes ethnographic research suggests small changes that can make the difference between a product succeeding in its market or falling flat.* (line 99)

A: The text mentions the cost of the research but does not say it will reduce costs.

B: The text says the research is agenda-less but not that it says how a product will perform.

C: The text mentions that a small number of people participate but not that they are likely to buy the product.

20 B: *London Business School even devotes its latest MBA core module – discovering entrepreneurial opportunities – to expounding the principles of ethnographic research* (line 114)

A: The text says it uses *only ethnographic and qualitative research* (line 125) i.e. two methods.

C: The text says students use this method but not that they must use it.

D: The text says that companies use this method but not that they advise the School to do so.

p16–17 READING Part Four

Questions 21–30

0 D: *spread* = expanded (in use); *unfolded* = opened or revealed; *widened* = become wider (physically); *displayed* = showed

21 B: *functional* = useful, fit for its purpose; *constructive* refers to an idea or suggestion or action that is helpful or likely to produce good results; *active* refers to something that is still working in a way that is normal or expected (e.g. a virus); *operative* usually refers to a machine that is working

22 A: *perishable* is used for food and items which go off or decay and can then no longer be used; *short-lived* = an experience or event that does not last long; *decaying* describes something that is already becoming destroyed; *destructible* is usually used for machines or objects that can be damaged. It is usually used it in its negative form i.e. *indestructible*

23 D: *industry* refers to businesses of a particular type; *manufacturers* refers to producing goods (not raw material); *enterprise* refers to a single organisation or business; *commerce* refers to trade in general

24 B: *establish … as* (something) = to set up something so that it continues; *install* = put in a piece of electrical equipment; *create* = make a product or system; *demonstrate* = show how something works

25 C: price *plans* = ways of buying goods or services; *designs* refers to the way something is made; *programmes* are plans or schedules for the future; *systems* = ways of doing something

26 B: *on* offer = *available*; *at* a particular offer; *for* a special offer, to be *under* offer = an offer to buy is being considered

27 D: *response* = a reaction to something that happens or is said; *return* = give something back or to answer someone; *retort* = quick or humorous spoken reply to something; *reply* = an answer to something spoken – in this sense this is not appropriate because something was not said

28 A: economic *downturn* = collocation; *downturn* in the economy; *fall* or *decrease* or *drop in* share value

29 **C:** to *do* without = to manage without something (NB intransitive); the other verbs are all transitive so require an object – *make* something without something; *carry* something without something; *stay* without something

30 **A:** to bring a/any *return* on something, e.g. an investment – this is a fixed phrase = to make a profit; to make a *gain* of x amount; to have an *interest* in something, e.g. a business; to make a *profit* of x amount

----

Further practice and guidance (p18–19)

A detailed study

1 1   to keep them up to date

   2   with a wireless vertical data business/ in Sweden

   3   Wall Street traders, business people, self-employed professionals

   4   It is being used by a wider market.

   5   an economic downturn

   6   make itself indispensable; prove it can bring a return on profit

2 1   A – 3; B – 1; C – 4; D – 2

   2   A – 4; B – 2; C – 1; D – 3

   3   A – 2; B – 4; C – 3; D – 1

   4   A – 2; B – 3; C – 4; D – 1

3 1   A – 2; B – 3; C – 1; D – 4

   2   A – 2; B – 4; C – 1; D – 3

   3   A – 3; B – 4; C – 2; D – 1

----

p20 READING Part Five

Questions 31–40

0   NOT: missing connector – *not* refers forward to *will also* in the next sentence, i.e. the connecting phrase *not only/just … but also*

31 AND: missing connector – *and* because two points are listed (cost of venue, whether participants are being charged) so this connects them

32 ARE: missing auxiliary – *are* because verb is *to be charged*

33 TO: missing infinitive of purpose – here *to* = *in order to*

34 FROM: missing word in fixed phrase – *from time to time* = occasionally

35 THESE: missing determiner – *These* refers back to the rooms in the previous sentence

36 TO: missing *to*- infinitive – *advise + not + to*-infinitive

37 ANY: missing word in fixed phrase – *in any case* = whatever happens

38 HOW: missing adverb – *how (many)* = what number

39 WHO/THAT: missing defining pronoun – *who* or *that* because *were overseas* defines which managers; *who* because it refers to people (i.e. managers)

40 SO: missing word in fixed phrase – *and so on* = etcetera

p21 READING Part Six

Questions 41–52

0   CORRECT

00 BECAUSE: this is wrong because it is not followed by a reason but by a description

41 THEIR: *their* makes *services* possessive but we don't know what these services are so we need to say *services* in general, i.e. without a determiner or pronoun

42 GOING: the correct phrase is *to be in talks with*; confusion with *going to talk* or *going to be in talks*

43 CORRECT

44 SUCH: *such* needs to have an adjective and noun (not a bare noun) and in this structure the noun should be followed by *that* … . This is not the case here. Confusion with *such a high price tag that* … .

45 FOR: *growth capital* is a compound noun and *necessary* is the adjective so there is no preposition between them; confusion with *provide the necessary* + noun (e.g. *input*) *for growth*

46 CORRECT

47 DESPITE: This would need to be *Despite the fact that* ... to be grammatically correct and this would not be correct with the meaning of *but* in the next line.

48 CORRECT

49 UP: *turnover has doubled* over the last three years; confusion with *We only have one desk so you will have to double up.* = share

50 WAS: *introduced* is active not passive here, i.e. Evans introduced Active to the Board; confusion with *Evans was introduced to Active by the Board.*

51 THAT: the post of Chairman describes the role; *that of* is a reference to something mentioned previously; confusion with *The Director's role will be taken by Mr Smith and that of Chairman will be taken by Mr Brown.*

52 TO: *will join*: confusion with *is also to join*

p22 WRITING Part One

Sample answer:

In 2002 employees at Site A worked an average of 35 hours a week and at Site B 37 hours per week. This was reflected in production where at Site A 300,000 units were produced but Site B produced more at 350,000 units. In 2004 working hours at Site A increased slightly by 2 hours whereas at Site B they remained the same. As a result of this change, units produced at Site A increased dramatically to 400,000 while holding at 300,000 at Site B. In 2006 both sites increased their average working hours so that at Site A average hours per week rose to 41 and slightly increased to 38 hours per week at Site B. However, both Site A and Site B produced the same amount of units at 420,000 meaning Site B had higher productivity. (138 words)

The report compares hours worked with output: *This was reflected in production where at Site A 300,000 units were produced but Site B produced more at 350,000 units.*

The report also compares data across the two sites: *In 2004 working hours at Site A increased slightly by 2 hours whereas at Site B they remained the same.*

Further practice and guidance (p23–24)

A detailed study

1

going up	going down	staying the same
rose	dipped	stabilised
increased	declined	flattened out
climbed	decreased	held
soared	crashed	levelled off
rocketed	collapsed	steadied
bounced back	plunged	rallied
recovered		

The odd one out is 'fluctuated' as this shows a varied movement.

2

surprisingly; suddenly; generally; roughly; considerably; dramatically; slowly; significantly; steadily; fairly; approximately; virtually

smooth, fast and *nice* cannot be used to refer to rises and falls in this way

3

Degree of change	Speed of change
dramatically	rapidly
sharply	swiftly
substantially	quickly
considerably	gradually
significantly	steadily
slightly	slowly
fairly	suddenly
	fast

4 3, 1, 5, 2, 4

First it is essential you understand the data and the instructions. (3,1)

Then you need to organise or plan your writing. (5)

When writing you must make sure you use advanced level language to express yourself. (2)

It is important to check your writing for any mistakes. (4)

5 1 This description is very simplistic and does not show a range of language.

  2 This description is best as it has complex clauses and a range of vocabulary. It also makes a complex comparison.

  3 This description is satisfactory but is rather pedestrian in the way it makes a comparison and uses too many percentages.

6 1 No – it needs to be about 30 words longer. This can be achieved by making more complex comparisons.

  2 Not really – you are asked to compare performance. This report just states the differences.

  3 *In this time* (line 3): we don't know what this is referring to

  4 *in average* (line 2) = on average, *remaindered* (line 5) = remained

  5 *which was good* (line 2) = delete, as you should not give your personal opinion in a report like this; *made about* (last line) = *produced*

p25 WRITING Part Two

Make sure you only write ONE of the choices.

The Part 2 task will be assessed on these criteria. Check your writing by answering the following questions:

- Content: Have you included all the points in the instructions?

- Organisation and cohesion: Is your answer balanced or have you written too much on one point? Have you used paragraphs appropriately? Have you used linking words so the reader can follow what you are saying? Have you used an appropriate layout?

- Register: Have you used formal language consistently and appropriately?

- Accuracy: Is all your vocabulary and grammar accurate? Is your spelling correct?

- Range: have you used a variety of structures and vocabulary to show you have advanced level language?

- Target reader: What effect would your writing have on the target reader? Would it be positive or would they be confused?

For further practice on reports, see page 51.

For further practice on letters, see page 79.

For further practice on proposals, see page 105.

p26 LISTENING Part One

Questions 1–12

1 *terms of reference: get your superior's approval for … what are referred to as 'the terms of reference'.* The answer is not 'drafts' as these are only initial versions rather than the final document. NB 'so-called' in the question matches 'what are referred to as' in the recording. These phrases indicate that you are expected to write down the phrase or word, often a name or a title, precisely as the speaker says it.

2 *progress: establish … break points … so you'll be able to monitor progress.*

3 *contribution(s):* team members can *start thinking how their contribution can best be made.* The answer is not 'ownership' as this is acquired not planned.

4 *timeline: you can then track them* (the different assignments) *against a timeline.*

5 *suppliers: problems … if suppliers withhold goods because their invoices haven't been paid.*

6 *contingency budget: a contingency budget will allow you to … cope with any unforeseen issue when it occurs.*

7 *written outline:* not 'role' as this would not fit with *of what's required of them.* The written outline provides details of the role.

8 *freedom: how much* is a clue as the speaker says some innovative people need **complete** freedom, while inexperienced staff want **less**. The answer is not 'impetus' as this cannot be quantified.

9 *praise: all staff need praise.* The answer is not 'morale' as the speaker is suggesting that praise increases confidence i.e. morale.

10 *face to face:* not 'by email'. The speaker says email is *fine for everyday stuff but important news needs to be given face-to face.*

11 *(careful) records: keep careful records of everything.*

12 *review: hold a review meeting with the team to reflect on your successes.* The answer is not 'budget' – the speaker is talking about the project arriving 'on budget' i.e. at the right price.

Further practice and guidance (p27–28)

A detailed study

Initial prediction

1   verb e.g. *understand*

2   noun e.g. *specifications*

3   noun e.g. *household names*

4   number – percentage e.g. *5.5%*

5   adjective e.g. *nationwide*

6   number – money e.g. *£15*

7   noun – e.g. *record-keeping*

8   verb e.g. *changed*

More detailed prediction

1   noun – plural e.g. *dates*. The clue to the plural = 'are changed'.

2   verb – infinitive e.g. *adapt*. The clue = 'need to'.

3   number – date e.g. *1995*. The clue is 'until'.

4   uncountable noun – singular e.g. *notice*. The clue is 'much'.

5   verb – past participle e.g. *replaced*. The clue is 'going to be'.

6   number – amount of money e.g. *£10,000*. The clue is 'an investment of'.

7   noun – singular e.g. *period*. The clue is 'a'.

8   number – time period e.g. *6 weeks*. The clue is 'it only took'.

9   verb – 'ing' form e.g. *developing*. The clue is 'look forward to'.

10   noun – title of member of staff e.g. *Training Officer*. The clue is 'spoke to'.

Reformulation

Question 4

'analytical software' = 'Critical Path Analysis' + 'computer + program'

'individual tasks' = 'different assignments'

'check' = 'track'

The type of word required = a singular noun and the answer is 'timeline'

Question 11

'are maintained' = 'keep'

'in case complications arise later'= 'if something goes wrong, you'll need to analyse why it happened'

The type of word required = a plural noun and the answer is 'records'.

p29 LISTENING Part Two

Questions 13–22

13   **E:**   … *the one last week. The objective was to settle what to attempt in the next twelve months and agree who should undertake which elements*

14   **F:**   … *we have our individual achievements and failures examined and receive feedback. My last boss used to … make some vague comments about my work*

15   **H:**   *These meetings where we analyse the pros and cons of possible additions to our range… junior staff … give short presentations on the proposed models*

16   **D:**   *Finding the right person to appoint is tricky as you've got to consider how they'd fit in with the rest of the team*

17   **B:**   *Our aim for the day was to work out some more favourable conditions on the bid we'd put in to develop a large site for them. We … had to accept tighter deadlines than we'd like*

18   **H:**   … *the MD insisted on going through what we'd committed to and checking our understanding of our contributions*

19   **E:**   *My last boss used to … shuffle through papers, which he was clearly looking at for the first time, and make some vague comments about my work. … This time, though, the new guy had made a comprehensive chart of my sales totals*

20   **G:**   … *it was the way it had been organized – a number of short points which needed active participation straight after lunch, while the more complex stuff had been discussed fully first thing*

21   **A:**   … *our Head of Department … she's not a great chair… she isn't firm enough so one or two people tend to take over*

22   **D:**   *I blame AER's Manager actually. He kept allowing people to raise issues that had no bearing on the matter in hand and this made us lose focus*

p30–31 LISTENING Part Three

Questions 23–30

23 C: *I felt I ought to experience the cut and thrust of the 'real world'*

A: He mentions that his father was an accountant and he had always been around figures, but he does not suggest he wanted to do the same job.

B: He says he thought about 'becoming a university tutor' and he valued 'college life and the prospect of doing research', so there is no suggestion that he wanted to escape an academic environment.

24 A: *I realise that the job was like that suit. I was too entrepreneurial to fit in somewhere where I had to take orders from people, particularly if I didn't respect them.*

B: He mentions that he bought a new suit with his first paycheck, but he doesn't say that he was desperate to earn money.

C: He wore his father's suit but does not suggest that this showed he was making an effort to fit in. He just didn't have a suit of his own.

25 C: *I wouldn't have got where I am now without it, that's for sure.*

A: There is no mention of studying for qualifications. He mentions 'a steep learning curve'.

B: He says that the 'hugely cutthroat atmosphere', gave him 'a real buzz' rather than a negative feeling.

26 A: *I was getting stale – I'd absorbed everything there was to know*

B: He mentions that if he'd stayed he would have made 'some serious money'.

C: He doesn't mention using his work contacts, only that he wants to follow his own dreams rather than realising other people's dreams

27 B: *What's different is that I've got a facility which I call a 'refuge', where entrepreneurs can come and explore different possibilities before starting up on their own.*

A: He says he does conference sessions on the 'stock variety of topics' i.e. the usual ones.

C: He says 'my main strand is helping self-employed people grow their businesses with the power of the internet, something that's hardly original now'.

28 C: *The web's just so vast now, that keeping abreast of the innovations is more than I can cope with.*

A: He doesn't need to persuade business people to use social networking sites because they're 'everywhere' and 'crucial in the business world'.

B: There is no suggestion that he finds it hard to maintain his interest in the internet. The innovations he talks about suggest that it is still fascinating.

29 B: *People would be much better off focusing on what they're good at and what turns them on and then trying to combine these two things*

A: He says that people should only work out a business plan when they have done some market research.

C: The market research should be carried out once the idea has been worked out.

30 A: *It took me ages to grasp that time's the real currency and making every second count's the key. Look out for something that makes you want to leap out of bed in the morning*

B: He mentions that he used to spend long hours working, but does not recommend how long people should spend working.

C: He does not advise on pay rates, only that people should choose something that excites them and perhaps they will be able to 'find ways to get paid well for doing it!'

p32 SPEAKING

> **Further practice and guidance (p33)**
>
> **A detailed study**
>
> | | | | |
> |---|---|---|---|
> | **(Q3)** | 1 | viii | H |
> | **(Q4)** | 2 | iv | D |
> | **(Q5)** | 3 | i | B |
> | **(Q6)** | 4 | v | E |
> | **(Q7)** | 5 | ii | A |
> | **(Q8)** | 6 | iii | C |
> | **(Q9)** | 7 | vii | G |

TEST 2

p36–37 READING Part One

Questions 1–8

0   **C:**   *potential 'Dream Team' people are not difficult to identify.*

1   **D:**   *Most important from the entrepreneur's point of view is to develop and maintain the right culture, which is essentially tribal.*

2   **E:**   *There's nothing wrong with an ambitious employee coming to a manager and saying they should be paid as much as someone else ...*

3   **A:**   *people should be praised for 'having a go'*

4   **C:**   *if people do not shape up they tend to be out of the revolving door quite quickly.*

5   **D:**   *It's important to have formal, six monthly reviews with agreed targets ...*

6   **A:**   *In every start-up there are many more jobs than people to do them.*

7   **E:**   *the wise entrepreneur gets advice and mentoring from people with specific expertise in the area ...*

8   **B:**   *This is also the perfect learning experience for those who have dreams of themselves becoming a cornerstone one day or even of starting their own company.*

p38–39 READING Part Two

Questions 9–14

0   **H:**   *Winning some production work on archived material of a BBC comedy series for her company Ascent Media set in motion **a connection that has now lasted more than a decade**.*

This sentence explains what happened in the previous sentence. The phrase *a connection that has now lasted more than a decade* links to *keeping a sales relationship long term* in the sentence after the gap.

9   **D:**   *She has worked for **the group** for 13 years, mostly in **sales**.*

She refers to *Ms Mitchells* in the previous sentence, *the group* refers to *Ascent Media* in the previous sentence. The word *sales* tells us what she does and refers forward to *best deal* in the sentence after the gap.

10   **G:**   *"The UK TV industry is a very social industry and **everyone seems to know each other**," she says.*

The phrase *everyone seems to know each other* refers forward to *bump into* in the sentence following the gap.

11   **A:**   *She kindly agreed to give me some details of **this lady**.*

She refers to *a client* in the previous sentence; *this lady* refers to the *head of production* in the previous sentence. The word *she* in the sentence after the gap refers to *this lady*.

12   **C:**   *It turned out that VCI was doing **a lot of work** repackaging media content.*

It turned out refers to *what she was doing* mentioned in the previous sentence. *The work* in the sentences following the gap refers back to *a lot of work*.

13   **F:**   *This initial work went on and the relationship between the companies deepened. More than a decade later, **they still work together**.*

This initial work refers to *first programmes* and *repackaging content* referred to in the previous sentences. The sentence after the gap gives the details of how the long relationship (*they still work together*) was maintained.

14   **E:**   *One of the things that's been vital is that we spent a lot of time giving **her** company staff training and technical training because the industry **changes** rapidly with emerging technologies.*

One of the things that's been vital refers to how we could support her in the previous sentence. The word *her* refers to the *head of production* in the previous sentence (established as *her* in the earlier text). There is also reference to *changes* in the sentence after the gap.

Choice B: *However, Ms Mitchells' relationship is still going strong.*

There is no place in the text where this sentence would fit.

Further practice and guidance (p40–41)

A detailed study

1 e, i, a, g, c, h, b, f, d

2 **1** *this* refers to the situation of a TV comedy programme beginning a business relationship.

   2 *where there* refers to the film production industry

   3 *she* refers to Ms Mitchells

   4 *She* refers to the client in the previous sentence.

   5 *she* refers to the head of production in the previous sentence.

   6 *the trio* refers to Ms Mitchells, her former client and the head of production at VCI.

   7 *The work* refers to the repackaging of media content just mentioned.

   8 *that* refers to the help with production just mentioned.

3 **1** – c (*it* refers back to the situation; *although* needs a contrast)

   2 – e (*his* refers to the director; *so* is a result/consequence, often of a problem)

   3 – f (*the issue* refers back to *the problem*)

   4 – a (*more* refers back to content of sessions; *By + -ing* … requires a logical conclusion)

   5 – d (*those + n't* refers back to *not everyone*; this is two separate sentences)

   6 – b (*However* refers back to 'some' i.e. it deals with the remainder)

4 **A** The Head of Production at VCI. We know she is *this lady* as the sentence after the gap refers to her receiving lots of calls.

   B A previously mentioned problem or contrast with what follows. This is the distractor and does not fit into a gap in the text.

   C The result of the situation and/or problems that the lady at VCI described.

   D This extract gives her name, age, job and company which shows it is an introduction so we can expect it to appear in an appropriate place e.g. near the beginning.

   E The one between the speaker and the head of production at VCI.

   F A description, explanation or example of the work they do now.

   G An example of the situation she has described.

p42–43 READING Part Three

Questions 15–20

15 **B:** *It is all about creating a dialogue with them, and that works in favour of customer magazines.* (line 16)

   A: The text talks about traditional magazines but does not say whether or not people no longer want to read them.

   C: The text says the opposite of this, i.e. that companies want to keep existing customers.

   D: The text talks about new marketing techniques but does not mention which particular businesses they were needed for.

16 **C:** *some detractors claiming that customer magazines are the marketing equivalent of the wolf in sheep's clothing – a cynical sales tool purporting to be a glossy magazine.* (line 26)

   A: The text discusses the purpose of the articles but not the quality. In fact, it implies the articles are quite good.

   B: The text does not mention advertising. In fact the early part of the text explains they are editorially driven (even though they are 'selling' something).

   D: The text does not mention charging for the magazines.

17 **D:** *The whole debate now is how we can get customers reading in a more exciting way* (line 45)

   A: The text says that this is already taking place, not that new developments will take place (see question) in this area.

   B: The text talks about increasing interest in the websites, not magazines.

   C: The text talks about companies exploiting their technology but not that new developments will take place to deal with this.

18 A: *However some publishing executives believe that the sector is getting "carried away" with digital and experiential marketing. "We have spent the past two years proving the success of customer magazines and, what, are we supposed to abandon ship now and say 'Well actually digital is the way forward?'"* (lines 56–62)

B: The text talks about the past not the future and not in this context.

C: The text does not comment on what techniques experiential marketing is appropriate for.

D: this is mentioned but not in the context of what some executives think (see question).

19 B: *the vast amount of Dunnhumby's findings are used to identify shopping patterns and trends in Tesco's stores.* (line 71)

A: The text says Tesco has a magazine but not that the card has any connection to the magazines.

C: The text particularly singles out Tesco as unusual here so it does not apply to some companies.

D: The text says that Tesco does respond quickly to customer needs but that is not the purpose of using the example of the card.

20 C: *The key element is getting the ranges right in the stores.* (line 85)

A: Dunn mentions that retailers are getting more communication with customers but not whether or not they would like this.

B: Dunn says *there is less need for fancy promotions* (line 81)

D: Dunn says that returning customers are important but does not mention whether or not they are more important than new customers.

p44–45 READING Part Four

Questions 21–30

0 D: *boss* = from the common expression 'to be your own boss'; *executive* is the person in charge of a company; *chief* indicates the most important rank in, for example, the police force – chief constable; *head* is often used in Head of Department, or Head of a college etc.

21 C: *fail* = when a business becomes insolvent or bankrupt; *fall* is used when prices or shares lose value; *subside* = sinking or going down; A person *resigns* from (gives up) his job.

22 B: *trading* = engage in commerce; *handling* can mean to manage as in 'he handles people well'; *establishing* means *setting up* and the verb needs a direct object e.g. a company; *transacting* means to conduct business. This verb also needs a direct object.

23 D: *deliver* = to hand over goods e.g. deliver the machinery to the buyer or to carry out a service; *consign* is only used for goods; *execute* means to perform a task as instructed; *fulfil* means to complete something as required e.g. to fulfil an order

24 C: *forecast* = in business terms this means to assess or to calculate beforehand; *foresee* is used in more general terms to guess that something will happen; *predict* means to foretell on the basis of present knowledge: *I predict that the market will rise next month*; *present* is used to introduce someone, give an award etc.

25 B: *promotion* = the act of encouraging the sales of a product; *advertisement* = a single piece of promotion on TV, in magazines etc.; *publication* = the act of publishing (issuing) a book or magazine; *press* = another term for the printed media – newspapers and magazines

26 D: *sources* = places or people where help or inspiration can be found; *representatives* are people who act for a company, often a sales representative; *agents* are people who are authorised to transact business for a company; *organisers* arrange events such as conferences.

27 A: *advisor* = person who provides advice on, for example, financial or legal matters; An *assistant* helps a higher ranking person carry out their duties; A *counsellor* gives advice on personal or psychological problems; A *backer* provides financial support for a business.

28 A: *generate* = often used in financial situations to mean to make money; *create* is used in more imaginative situations e.g. to create a new design; *develop* means to cause to grow or advance and is used with ideas, products, systems etc.; *cause* means to produce an effect, e.g. *cause a slump* in the market.

29 **D:** *viability* = a business has a prospect of surviving and succeeding; *practicality* means effectiveness e.g. the practicality of a system or a type of work clothing; *worth* means value in financial terms – how much a company is worth if it is being sold; *benefit* means an advantage and can also be a right to payment under a social security scheme.

30 **D:** *feedback* = the comments that are given by e.g. customers in a questionnaire; *analysis* is the process of examining data; *talkback* is a two-way radio system; *judgement* is an opinion and can be a legal conclusion.

p46 READING Part Five

Questions 31–40

0 UP: missing preposition in phrasal verb *set up* = to establish

31 AT: missing preposition in fixed phrase *at some point*

32 SUCH: missing adjective in phrase *such as*, meaning for example

33 TO: missing preposition in fixed phrase *according to* meaning as stated by

34 LEAST: missing superlative adjective in collocation *at least* meaning a minimum

35 OR: missing conjunction that refers back to *whether*: *whether a or b*

36 WITH: missing preposition that collocates with *come* to mean is accompanied by

37 A: missing article in fixed phrase *as a rule of thumb* meaning as a general rule.

38 AS: missing adverb following the verb *to view*

39 ON: missing preposition that collocates with *site*

40 LESS: missing comparative adjective to indicate that it is not so likely that homeworkers' houses will be broken into

---

Further practice and guidance (p47)

A detailed study

1   1   relative pronoun – *who / that*
    2   auxiliary verb – *have*
    3   comparison – *more*
    4   article – *the*
    5   preposition – *in*
    6   conjunction – *but*

2   1   as
    2   other
    3   of
    4   the
    5   but
    6   for

---

p48 READING Part Six

Questions 41–52

0 CORRECT

00 FOR: The verb 'provide' takes a direct object – *the company provides a bus to the town centre*

41 AT: No preposition is needed after 'perceive'.

42 CORRECT

43 WITH: You integrate one thing into another existing system so the preposition is not needed.

44 OF: *Total* in this case is an adjective not a noun, so *of* is unnecessary.

45 THAT: The 'ing' form of the verb 'cover' is describing the reporters so no relative pronoun is needed.

46 CORRECT

47 HOWEVER: *However* is used to introduce a contradiction or a change of direction. This is not the case here as the writer is continuing to describe the people who communicate with the press.

48 AS: *As* is used to introduce a comparison between two people, groups or objects. Here no direct comparison is being made.

49 MOST: *Most* would be needed if the writer was stating which medium was top in some way, but he is not providing that information.

50 THEREFORE: *Therefore* means 'for that reason', but there is no reason given for choosing the chief executive in the previous line.

51 CORRECT

52 ARE: The expression is 'to make someone available for ...' so the auxiliary verb is not needed.

p49 WRITING Part One

Sample answer:

Over the four-year period of 2005–2008 sales generally have risen. Between 2005 and 2006 there was an overall rise in sales, though the bulk of sales were at home and only a small percentage abroad. In 2005 much more was spent on advertising and marketing at home than abroad. Overall there was only a very small rise in sales in 2007 though there was a greater proportion of sales abroad in this year. In 2008 total sales rose dramatically principally because there was a significant rise in sales abroad. Sales at home remained steady. This was despite the fact that proportionally more was still spent on sales and marketing at home than abroad. So it would appear that sales abroad are strong and rising without requiring increased advertising or marketing investment.

(133 words)

The report compares advertising and marketing with sales:

*   there was an overall rise in sales

*   the bulk of sales were at home and only a small percentage abroad

*   there was only a very small rise in sales in 2007 though there was a greater proportion of sales abroad in this year

*   This was despite the fact that proportionally more was still spent on sales and marketing at home than abroad.

The report also reaches a conclusion about the data:

*   So it would appear that sales abroad are strong and rising without requiring increased advertising or marketing investment.

p50 WRITING Part Two

Question 2: report

Sample answer:

<u>Aim</u>

The aim of this report is to assess the success of the recent programme to save energy and recycle waste and to suggest what improvements could be made.

<u>The measures the Administration department has taken</u>

In the Administration department we have dramatically reduced photocopying by asking staff to reconsider whether they need hard copies of certain forms and information. We have also introduced a centralised system whereby we only keep one hard copy in a file for all staff to refer to rather than each member of staff keeping their own files. In addition to this, we have also asked maintenance to replace all the lighting with low energy bulbs and will be monitoring the cost of this over the next few months.

<u>An evaluation of the success of the programme</u>

Staff are very keen to assist in this programme so we are optimistic that any measures we do institute will be followed appropriately and cost savings will be made. We have already seen this in a reduced photocopying bill. So far we have not made much progress with a recycling programme.

<u>Suggested improvements</u>

It is vitally important that we not only seek new ways of saving energy and recycling waste but that we are able to monitor the effectiveness of the programme. We would suggest that a member of staff is given sole responsibility within each department so that they can maintain an overview of the programme and its success and make changes where necessary.

(246 words)

The report:

- covers all the content points in the question (see section headings)

- is correctly organised and laid out, i.e. with headings

- uses formal language, e.g. to assess, use of the passive (e.g. *will be followed*), *that any measures we do institute, we not only seek …*, etc.

Further practice and guidance (p51–52)

A detailed study

1　All of them except 4 and 7; your opinion should be based on fact and you must always use formal and objective language.

2　2　Yes, e.g. how a system works, why something was done in a particular way, what a set of data means, etc.

　　3　Not likely to be part of a report because report is usually commissioned by someone for an assessment of something. (see page 105 on proposals)

　　4　May be included at the end of a report but is not the main focus, e.g. improvements, whether a new system or process should be adopted and/or extended etc.

　　5　Yes, e.g. functions, aims or purposes of the report

　　6　Not likely to be part of a report (see page 105 on proposals)

　　7　Yes, e.g. how well something was done, how effective a system is, etc

3　1　The language in this is too informal and the content is too simplistic. It does not summarise the whole purpose of the report.

　　2　This sentence is reasonably satisfactory but is expressed in simple structures and is not objective enough (e.g. *we*).

　　3　This is the best sentence. It is expressed in complex, objective language and summarises the purpose of the report.

4　1　a is more informal – it uses a personal pronoun rather than the passive; a also has a more complex clause structure (*when making*)

　　2　a is more formal – b uses emotive language (*not easy*) rather than the more objective and toned down *problematic*

　　3　b is more informal – it uses the subjective *I think* and also gives the purpose of the suggestion after the suggestion. This is reversed in a, where the purpose (reminding) is given first, and the passive voice is used (were reminded).

5　1　offers

　　2　It would be advisable to

　　3　It was successful.

　　4　Waste paper was separated for re-use.

　　5　… implemented a system …

6　1　The formality is inconsistent. The passive is used appropriately at the start but it concludes with a subjective opinion.

　　2　There is some rather simplistic language which reduces range e.g. The expression '… everyone was doing as they were told' could be expressed as '… all staff were following procedures'.

　　3　The focus starts well but the final sentence is not appropriate in the section to describe the measures taken. The task does not ask students to express their feelings.

　　4　It is accurate.

　　5　The heading 'What measures?' is unclear, though it is correct that it is underlined. This could be better expressed as 'Measures that were taken in the department'.

p53 LISTENING Part One

Questions 1–12

1 *event programme / program:* ... *pay to have a piece about Magnum printed in what's called 'the event programme'.* The answer is not 'national or local press', because the speaker says he is not convinced that is worth paying for.

2 *budget: Talking of money, we also work out a budget beforehand*

3 *image: you have to choose something that'll transmit an appropriate image of the company, and I think this glass paper weight will do that.*

4 *projector: check the projector's OK. We must remember to take a back-up for that, just in case it stops working.* The answer is not 'laptops' as each person will be taking one of those.

5 *badge: we've had a special badge printed for each of you.*

6 *breaks: We always have a rota so everyone gets breaks to prevent them falling asleep.*

7 *back: we'll display ours* (brochures) *right at the back.* The answer is not 'front' as this is a position which the speaker says leads to wasting brochures.

8 *eye contact: keep eye contact as that engages the visitor more.* The answer is not 'business card' as that does not fit with the verb 'maintain'.

9 *(carrier) bag: if they're struggling with armfuls of other promotional material you could offer a carrier bag. I've had some specially printed this year with the Magnum name.* The answer is not 'bottle of water' as this is for thirsty visitors rather than overburdened ones.

10 *debriefing: we have a debriefing just to assess what worked and what didn't.* The answer is not 'dinner' as this would not help them to 'review everything'.

11 *targets: to measure how we did with relation to the targets we set months ago.*

12 *leads: it'll be time to pursue all the leads we got.*

p54 LISTENING Part Two

Questions 13–22

13 **G:** *to look at how the product range was presented, you know, colour of the wrapping, visuals, type of print and so on. After some*

thought we suggested that and management agreed.

14 **E:** *we wrote a factual piece instead, emphasising the new more eco-friendly aspects of the model and invited people from the national and specialist papers to headquarters to see it.*

15 **D:** *we ... helped fund some local events. Obviously our name appeared on the programmes and in the venues.*

16 **H:** customers *receive a communication regularly, filled with information about changes in the firm and tips related to the products*

17 **B:** *so we tried something different – cardboard bins by the checkouts with small packets of chocolates...*

18 **F:** *over 60% of respondents thought the sauces tasted different and suspected we'd used real tomatoes instead of tomato flavouring.*

19 **C:** *We decided that something that appears in an article is considered more trustworthy than the best designed publicity material*

20 **A:** *it was clear in the next few months that consumers of our services were considerably less mature*

21 **G:** *her idea was that customers would buy more if they sat down and really examined what we offered carefully. When we tried out her proposal, sales did increase and a telephone survey revealed that was the reason*

22 **D:** *customer surveys suggested that people thought of it as suitable for very special occasions... Lots of new customers across the age range started to buy them, mainly at weekends.*

Further practice and guidance (p55–56)

A detailed study

Reformulation

Speaker 1

Task One answer = option G: 'improved packaging'. This is expressed in the tapescript as *colour of the wrapping, visuals, type of print and so on.* Other phrases that indicate the area of packaging include *how the product range was presented* and *we suggested that ...*

Task Two answer = option F: 'Customers thought the quality of the product ingredients had improved.' This is expressed in the tapescript as *over 60% of respondents thought the sauces tasted different and suspected we'd used real tomatoes instead of tomato flavouring.*

Distraction

Other Task One options referred to by Speaker 1:

a mailshot (option A: 'direct mailing')

a money-off coupon (option F: 'special offers')

Another Task Two option referred to by Speaker 1:

create a younger … image (option A: 'the average age of customers on our database decreased.'

Speaker 4

Task One answer = option H: 'a company newsletter'. This is expressed in the tapescript as … *receive a communication regularly filled with information about changes in the company and tips related to the products.*

Task Two answer = option G: 'People took more time to consider the product range.' This is expressed in the tapescript as … *sat down and really examined what we offered carefully.*

Other Task One options referred to by Speaker 4:

our website…presence on web directories (option C: 'website listing')

publicity offers sent by companies (option A: 'direct mailing')

Another Task Two option referred to by Speaker 4:

however much we improve the way products are presented (option E: 'Customers found the information was much clearer than before')

Words which rule out other options in Speaker 4:

I expected it to be internet-related – not that I'm against that. Lots of sales come through our website and our presence on web directories. No, her idea was that customers would buy more if they sat down and really examined what we offered carefully.

She believes people only glance at publicity offers sent by companies they use, however much they improve the way products are presented.

p57–58 LISTENING Part Three

Questions 23–30

23 **B:** *it's really the people. If they don't trust the leadership or buy into the reason for change, it's a lost cause.*

  A: Frank says that managers fail by believing that organisations have to change, invent different systems.

  C: Frank suggests this has a bearing, but it is not the main reason.

24 **C:** Frank says it was *'alienating'* not to *'explain the rationale'*. Julia agrees by saying, *'that was part of the problem. We didn't feel involved.'*

  A: Julia says this, but Frank doesn't.

  B: Frank suggests this but Julia rejects the idea.

25 **C:** *Staff who are happy to go with the flow tend to prove their worth in these changing situations.*

  A: Frank suggests that highly creative people get upset when the systems they've designed have to be abandoned.

  B: Julia suggests this, but Frank rejects it – they *cling to the established order.*

26 **B:** *Often what a company has been most successful at can act as an obstacle as it has to be abandoned in the redefining of what the company needs to become in future.*

  A: Frank suggests that incremental change is easier to get used to because it builds on past performance.

  C: Frank doesn't mention this, although Julia suggest transformational changes must be painful for everyone.

27 **A:** *Rhetoric flows over them and isn't accepted unless it's backed up by actions.*

  B: Frank mentions formal speeches but suggests that managers spend too long on them.

  C: Frank mentions chats round the water cooler, but Julia doesn't.

28 **B:** *It's always preferable to win people over if you can.*

  A: Frank may believe this, but his story illustrates the value of persuasion over force.

C: There is power in the story, the wind, but it failed to manage change i.e. get the traveller to take his coat off. The sun's gentle persuasion did it.

29 C: *The contributions from my coursemates are absolutely first class and that's really helpful in discussions.*

A: Julia mentions that the course materials are good but says that some are out of date, so not very relevant.

B: Julia says that the tutors teach well and that they are 'quite approachable', so not **very** friendly.

30 B: Julia says, *What makes it for me is being able to give space to working through theories and evaluating them for myself.* Frank agrees when he says *You wouldn't think that'd be so valuable, would you, but it certainly is.*

A: Julia suggests this is useful, but she could always do it by herself. Frank disagrees.

C: Julia says the contacts are useful, but she could make them at work.

p60 SPEAKING

Further practice and guidance (p61–62)

Introduction
1 about
2 by
3 move
4 conclude/finish

Expressing your ideas
1 d
2 a
3 e
4 c
5 b
6 g
7 f

TEST 3

p64–65 READING Part One

Questions 1–8

0 E: *Brinkhoff and Thonemann found that managers' willingness and ability to approach and resolve conflicts constructively proved indispensable.*

1 C: *Top management support is vital in order to ensure that the necessary resources are provided* and *the whole thing worked because the managers of both enterprises were clearly and genuinely behind the project and its objectives.*

2 A: *In some cases, the teams actually performed as planned, but went off in different directions.*

3 E: *They have to be excellent communicators and motivators, and Brinkhoff and Thonemann found that managers' willingness and ability to approach and resolve conflicts constructively proved indispensable.*

4 B: *The people who actually work on the project must be convinced that any planned changes are necessary and appropriate.*

5 C: *This kind of positive interaction between project and line management can never be taken for granted.*

6 A: *This was solved early on in the process … well-communicated standardisation of packaging and quantities.*

7 D: *The inevitable lack of transparency and concealment that accompanies such relationships, generally leads to the collapse of the project.*

8 B: *Joint workshops, including both firms, provide a good solution. These entail not only communication on all elements of the project, but ensure the mutual development of change. This regular exchange of ideas also works wonders for motivation.*

p66–67 READING Part Two

Questions 9–14

0 H: *And more importantly, what's the answer to the question in the first place?*

the question refers back to the one asked in the previous sentence.

9 F: *But there's a lot of evidence to suggest that you can learn to be a good manager and there are particular practices you can put in place.*

But introduces a contradiction of the point of view that you can't make good managers in the previous sentence. The contradiction expressed here is that you can train people to manage. This sentence also, with the previous sentence, provides the input for Philpott's comments mentioned in the sentence after the gap. The *common frustration* referred to in the sentence after the gap is the fact that companies don't know if managers are born or made.

10 B: *The view is that management training certainly has an important role in developing further the managers who have it but the ones who don't are a lost cause.*

The view is refers to the view of potential clients mentioned in the previous sentence. This sentence gives an example of the result of the view that *managers are born and can't be made* in the previous sentence. The sentence after the gap explains the 'view' in even more detail.

11 E: *To manage individuals properly, **you have to be able to** identify their strengths and potential quickly and discover exactly how to talk and act with them to encourage them to work harder and better.*

This sentence gives details of what is meant by *demanding* in the previous sentence. *The ability to read other people* in the sentence after the gap refers to **you have to be able to** ...

12 A: *What is first required is a profound structural change in selecting managers and then in how they are deployed and **rewarded**.*

What is first required is a solution to the problem presented in the previous sentence. *their pay* in the sentence after the gap refers back to **rewarded**.

13 G: *Not only because managers would be focused on managing people well, but also because much better managerial candidates would put themselves forward in the first place.*

Not only because is an explanation of how management standards would improve, mentioned in the previous sentence. This system mentioned in the sentence after the gap refers back to the system explained in sentence G.

14 C: *It is therefore far easier to offer them management training courses predicated on the myth that you can make all those bad managers good.*

It is therefore far easier expresses the result of the view mentioned in the previous sentence. *In fact* in the sentence after the gap presents a contrast with this view.

Choice D: *Any ambitious individual who wants to ascend the corporate ladder almost always has to take on a management role first.*

There is no place in the text where this sentence would fit.

p68–69 READING Part Three

Questions 15–20

15 D: *So, the research concludes, the insufficient integration of personnel, organisational, technical and client-related processes, leads to the high flop rate.* (line 19)

A: The text talks about customers being willing *to buy innovative goods* etc., not that they are reluctant, so this is not a cause of failure.

B: The text says that companies may have little experience of technology or that it can be expensive, but not that they only invest a limited amount.

C: The text mentions costs but does not mention flexibility, nor does it mention costs as a reason for failure.

16 C: *The Hamburg group believes the vital initial phases of the innovation process have been neglected in both theory and practice.* (line 30)

A: The text says Hamburg believe that innovation may require a new process but not different processes.

B: The text says that Hamburg are suggesting an original approach (*in their own innovative way*) but not that it has failed or they believe that it has failed.

D: The text talks about the early phase but does not mention that the Hamburg group claim the process should be separated into different phases. The existence of different phases is already understood.

17 A: *In order to ensure internal support, people need to be convinced, and realistically so, of the real value of products and projects.* (line 43)

B: The text says communication/co-operation can prevent problems, not that it can resolve them.

C: The text says that budgets should be realistic and risks should be reduced – *A targeted reduction of technical and market uncertainty from the beginning further increases the chances of success* (line 38) – not that risks should be taken.

D: The text talks about whether plans are practicable but does not mention time.

18 **B:** *successful innovation is frequently the result, not of central planning, but of trial and error and the learning processes of groups of innovators given the freedom to operate as independent units.* (line 54)

A: The text talks about what typical managers do but not that they have inadequate training.

C: The text implies that risk taking is an advantage of smaller groups – *Prof. Kriegesmann believes in 'partisan wars' in which small groups within the firm develop innovative ideas contrary to the mainstream* (line 51) – not that it can be reduced.

D: Professor Kriegesmann suggests that planning works against innovation – *This is often not the case* (line 50) – not that it is needed.

19 **D:** *They often go 'underground' in companies and only emerge when they are convinced of success.* (line 65)

A: The text does not mention a variety of processes.

B: The text says they work a lot but does not say when.

C: The references to *'underground'* (line 66) means they work outside the mainstream of what is going on in the company, not that they are in a different location.

20 **C:** The answer to this comes from the main argument running through the text as a whole and is summarized in the last paragraph.

A: The focus of the text is about how to make innovation more successful not that too many products are failing. It mentions failure and the way to resolve this.

B: The text proposes that innovation often takes place outside normal company processes and should be dealt with differently so this statement is not a true summary.

D: The text mentions that the process of successful innovation has not yet been fixed and it makes some new suggestions about ways to approach innovation but the focus is not about the fact that we know very little about innovation.

Further practice and guidance (p70–71)

A detailed study

1 4, 2, 7, 1, 6, 3, 5

2 Question 15: paragraph 2 – *The reason for innovation glitches/according to recent research at the University of Bochum …*

Question 16: paragraph 3 – *the Hamburg group believes …*

Question 17: paragraph 4 – *this so-called 'fuzzy front-end' is where the foundations of the innovation process are laid*

Question 18: paragraph 5 – *Prof. Kriegesmann believes …* (it is established at the beginning of this paragraph that the Professor leads the Bochum team)

Question 19: paragraph 6 – *It is, therefore, ….*

Question 20: an overview of the whole text coupled with the main point in the conclusion (final paragraph)

4 1 insufficient integration (para 2)

2 been neglected (para 3)

3 people need to be convinced (para 4)

4 real value (para 4)

5 trial and error (para 5)

6 given the freedom to operate as independent units (para 5) and working in their own special way (para 6)

5 1 introduction

2 introduce

3 adaptation

4 adaptive/adapted

5 compatible

6 incompatible

7 be willing

8 willing

9 unwilling

10 proof

11 proven

12 unproven

13 solution

14 solvable

15 insoluble/insolvable/unsolved

16 target

17 target

18 specification

19 specify

20 unspecified

21 development

22 developed

23 undeveloped/underdeveloped

24 dynamism

25 undynamic

6 1 D   5 G

   2 H   6 B

   3 E   7 F

   4 A   8 C

p72–73 READING Part Four

Questions 21–30

0 C: *across* = location/across the length of; *over* = over a period of time; *along* = along a path/route; *among* = in the middle of (e.g. a group)

21 B: *drive* = effort e.g. an expansion drive; *an action* = usually a single action; *advance* = a move forward by an army; *surge* = a sudden move forward e.g. by a crowd

22 C: *giant* = very big organisation or multinational e.g. a retail giant; *colossus* = someone who is big or important; *monster* = something large but bad or frightening; *body* = a group of people e.g. the student body, a body of doctors, usually working together for a particular purpose

23 A: *in operation* = something is already in operation; *at* = in a particular place; *on* = in a particular position; *into* = to put into operation

24 D: *prevent* = actively stop something happening; *avoid* = manage to stop something or keep away from something;

check = to stop yourself from doing something; *restrain* = to hold someone to stop them doing something

25 C: *piloted* = to test a new idea or product on people to see if it will be successful; *proved* = when something has been tried and proved to be successful or not; *experimented* = to try a new idea, experimented with a new idea; *examined* = to look very carefully at something or to test somebody in an examination

26 A: *trade* = to buy and sell good and services; *deal* = to deal in goods and services or deal with someone; *transact* = to do business with someone (transitive); *traffic* = to buy and sell illegal goods

27 B: *range* = a variety of products; *class* = a type of product; *series* = a set of products that are of the same kind; *chain* = a set of shops or businesses

28 A: *generated* = produced or created; *caused* = caused to happen; caused by something; *formulated* = develop a plan or set of rules; *initiated* = to start a plan or process

29 D: *complete* = finish; *achieve* = succeed; *perform* = act; *settle* = decide or complete, to settle something (transitive)

30 C: *involving* = including; *containing* = holding; *concerning* = affecting; *covering* = dealing with a subject or group of things, usually used for a talk or course

p74 READING Part Five

Questions 31–40

0 SOME: missing determiner – *some* because we do not know or say exactly how much

31 TO: missing preposition – transitive sense so needs *to*

32 BE: missing verb – *be* = *it may be the case that*

33 THIS/SO: missing reference to what has gone before – *this* = *'visit the country'*, etc.

34 WITH: missing preposition – *along with somebody/something*

35 WHICH: missing reference to what has gone before i.e. *'during which time'*

36 IF: missing connector – *if* because what follows is a condition

37 WHAT: missing determiner – *what = the thing that*. Confusion with *It is strange that …* where *It* is a pronoun

38 THAT: missing pronoun in defining clause – necessary because it is the subject of the verb. NB *which* not possible c.f. *the fact/idea/ theory that …* .

39 NOT: missing negative – the sentence needs a negative to make sense in the context of the text

40 FROM: missing preposition – *to detract from* something

p75 READING Part Six

Questions 41–52

0   CORRECT

00 FOR: *attend an interview* not 'attend for'; confusion with **go for** an interview

41 CORRECT

42 HAD: This sentence needs to be in the present tense so *have ha*d is incorrect; confusion with e.g. *once they have had the job for a period of time then …* etc.

43 SO: *so* would need a result or conclusion after it, e.g. **so** *they don't worry about their clothes*; what follows is an activity

44 CORRECT

45 WHO: confusion with *people who are considered to be*

46 SUCH: confusion with *take such important factors as …* without a number and preceded or followed by a list

47 ARE: *they dress to fit in with*; confusion with *they are* **dressed** *to fit …* i.e. adjective

48 IN: *fit the image of* = be suitable; confusion with **fit in with** something = to be similar to

49 THE: *creativity* is used as an abstract noun or concept here, so does not have *the* before it; confusion with e.g. *the creativity which he showed in the task* i.e. specific creativity

50 THAN: *more individual clothes* (i.e. more individual than usual); confusion with the position of *than* in this context

51 CORRECT

52 THAT: *in this way, they begin*; confusion with *It is* in this way **that** *they begin to …*

Further practice and guidance (p76)

A detailed study

1 1   because their job may depend on the impression they create

   2   wear comfortable clothes

   3   people who consider what they wear to work

   4   dressing to fit the company image; dressing the same as the managers above them

   5   you need to think about how you dress at work if you want promotion

2 1 b *had*: (the clause after *so* is about him using the opportunities he has now so *had* (present perfect) is wrong here).

   2 b *who*: (*who* is not right without *are* so in this case this sentence should be: *People thought to be clever are promoted quickly.*)

   3 b *in*: (if you use *in*, then you must also have *with*, so in this case the sentence should be: *He doesn't fit the company image.*)

   4 a *the*: (in this sentence *power* is used as a concept so it is without the article; sentence b refers to specific power so using *the* is necessary)

   5 a *than*: (there is no comparative element after the *than* so it is incorrect)

3 1   *and*: this links the two clauses and there is no contrast so *Although* is incorrect.

   2   *so in this way*: there is no verb to introduce the *that-* clause so that is incorrect. If the sentence had read … *so it is in this way …* then *that* would have been correct.

   3   *If*: the second clause is the action suggested for the condition set in the first clause. *So* means what follows is a reason why, so it is not appropriate in this context.

   4   *by* etc.: *Because* would only be correct if what followed after *controlled* was a complete clause e.g. *you should be careful how you manage the budget.*

NB Remember punctuation can be important in deciding whether a word is extra or not.

p77 WRITING Part One

Sample answer:

Over the five-year period from 2004-2008 the cost of coal per ton generally increased. During that time the company's requirements for coal fluctuated. In 2005 the company costs rose from the previous year but the company demand for coal dropped significantly. In 2006 there was a sharp rise in the company's demand for coal and the cost rose slightly. The company's demand for coal continued to rise to a peak in 2007 but at this point the cost fell slightly. In 2008 the company bought substantially less coal. However, the cost per ton peaked for the period at $82 per ton. Over the same period their requirement for other fuels did not change but the cost of other fuels varied, rising in 2005 and 2006 and falling dramatically in 2007. This cost rose again slightly in 2008.

(139 words)

The report compares the costs and purchases of fuels as required in the instructions. It deals with coal and other fuels separately as this is clearer. It also uses summary sentences:

- Over the five-year period from 2004-2008 the cost of coal per ton generally increased. During that time the company's requirements for coal fluctuated.

- Over the same period their requirement for other fuels did not change but the cost of other fuels varied …

p78 WRITING Part Two

Question 3: The letter

Sample answer:

Dear Sir or Madam,

Our company is a major producer of office furniture located on the outskirts of Manchester. We have been operating for over fifty years and have branches across the country. We are writing to you because we have just won a new contract and are looking to recruit extra staff.

The new contract is to supply EnergyPlus with furniture at their new Head Office outside London. This is a significant contract and all the furniture will have to be ready by 30th September, two weeks before the office opens. In order to fulfil this contract on time, we need 10 extra staff to work full-time on the factory floor for a period of three months starting at the beginning of next month.

The staff should have operated wood turning machinery before and should have experience of assembling large pieces of furniture or equipment. They must also speak good English in order to understand the brief training session and health and safety instructions.

We are therefore looking to use an agency to advertise and interview staff and to make a final decision about who is appropriate. We will also require the agency to agree final terms with the staff and manage contracts. We would be prepared to agree this arrangement on a fee or commission basis. If your agency is able and willing to do this work we would be grateful if you could contact us to arrange a meeting.

Yours faithfully   (244 words)

1   The letter covers the three content points in the question:

- The new contract is to supply …

- The staff should have operated …

- We are therefore looking to use an agency to …

2   The layout and organisation is appropriate for a letter.

3   The language is appropriately formal as the addressee is unknown, e.g.

- are looking to recruit

- In order to fulfil this contract on time
- We would be prepared to agree this arrangement

4   The target reader would be adequately informed.

Further practice and guidance (p79–80)

A detailed study

1   b

2   c

3   6, 3, 1, 4, 5, 2

4   The following is a suggested plan:

1	need help recruiting staff
2	name of company; what it produces
3	what new contract is for; how long; what it involves
4	experience: worked with cutting tools skills: team work; speak English
5	advertise, interview, select and sort contracts
6	please contact … etc; look forward to … etc.

5   1   G, B, D, K

   2   E, A, I, L

   3   C, F, H, J

6   1   Content: 2 – The letter doesn't say what kind of work new staff need to have done before.

   2   Organisation: 2 – There is too little paragraphing. Start a new paragraph when you begin a new topic.

   3   Range and accuracy: 3 – The structures are accurate but the language is too simplistic.

   4   Register: 2 – it is too chatty and informal, e.g. use of contractions, 'many thanks'

   5   Effect on target reader: 2 – Would not be fully informed (see point 1) and may be offended by the over-familiar tone.

---

p81 LISTENING Part One

Questions 1–12

1   *shared vision*: *working out initially what I call a 'shared vision' of the best way the team could operate.* Note 'what I call' mirrors 'what Karen refers to as' in the question.

2   *leadership*: *It takes time and seasoned leadership expertise to encourage the team to … attain consensus on how to advance.*

3   *details*: *it also needs people who can focus on the details and spot any complications before they arise.* The answer is not 'complications' as this matches 'problems' in the question.

4   *weakness*: *they'll also be expected to try to make up for whatever weakness arises in the team.* The answer is not 'strengths' as you do not need to compensate for those.

5   *stakeholders*: *you shouldn't only think about the external customers, there are others who are concerned in the outcome of your work, … So check who these stakeholders are.* The answer is not 'customers', 'senior management' or 'suppliers' as these are individual groups of interested people, while the question focuses on 'the whole range', which is the stakeholders in general.

6   *sponsors*: *I like to call this group the 'sponsors', and you'll need to update them regularly on developments.*

7   *team spirit*: *group activities help to create team spirit.*

8   *progress*: *a group lunch on Fridays. This would enable you to assess progress in an informal atmosphere.*

9   *trust*: *Things like this can help to foster a mood of trust between team members.* The answer is not 'efficiency' as this paraphrases 'work will go better' in the question.

10   *interpersonal issues*: *be on the look out for any interpersonal issues. Deal with them quickly.*

11   *blame*: *establish early on that the team is not a place where a culture of blame can be tolerated.*

12   *gossip*: *all workplaces are alive with gossip… it can …create divisions in a team, which you certainly don't want, so keep it to a minimum.* The answer is not 'human interaction' as that is not something that a team leader wants to restrict and it wouldn't fit with 'about members of the team'.

p82 LISTENING Part Two

Questions 13–22

13 H: *What was making me uneasy, though, was the courier – the marketing brochures hadn't been delivered and I only had a few with me.*

14 G: *Above all, I was uneasy about the people marketing had targeted with their mailshot – I wasn't convinced they'd focused on the right profile.*

15 E: *I wasn't convinced that I'd got the organisation of my talk right. I wanted to emphasise the positive benefits ... and so I spent most of the time on that aspect. It could have appeared **a bit one-sided** (not balanced).*

16 B: *I'd chosen a more artistic font for my slides and I was convinced things wouldn't be legible from the back.*

17 C: *I was in two minds whether to go to Australia recently for a congress... you have to weigh up whether these events are worth the costs in terms of travel, accommodation and time too. I wasn't at all convinced.*

18 E: *someone from the New York Times came and he wrote a complimentary piece about our new range.*

19 H: *the head of HR at Grants, the international pharmaceutical company, contacted me later. We met and he's recommending our top-of-the-range policy to his board.*

20 A: *after some discussion in the group, my recommendation was accepted.*

21 F: *someone who works for a company with ... upmarket hotels ... wanted to talk about the possibility of us running some sessions for their junior managers, focusing on customer relations and better communications. That's all fixed now.*

22 C: *a newspaper group want to relocate into a state-of-the-art building and he suggested we put in a bid to design it.*

p83–84 LISTENING Part Three

Questions 23–30

23 B: *... emotion. That comes through body language and tone of voice, and without it, co-operation on projects, for example, is jeopardised in my view.*

A: Clare is not concerned about the use of emails. She says *electronic messages are unparalleled for conveying facts fast*, but they don't convey emotion.

C: She mentions the number of voicemails – *voicemails clog our phones daily* – but not their sound quality. She goes on to mention *tone of voice* but in relation to face-to-face conversation.

24 A: James says meetings are an opportunity to find out where the other person's coming from. Clare agrees by saying *I couldn't agree more. Take a meeting I had with trades union representatives ... By hearing them out first ... I managed to defuse the situation and move on*

B: James says that seeing meetings *as a chance to get their own point across* is not a good idea. Clare does not mention it.

C: Clare says that *repeating the management line* doesn't work. James does not mention this.

25 C: *this makes them feel they belong to the group and I think that's crucial to the successful working of a unit and indirectly to the organisation.*

A: He suggests people express their views at internal meetings but they are unlikely to be acted on.

B: He suggests that management could keep people informed more easily by memo.

26 A: *Someone joining our company alienated his colleagues by always sending memos, which were seen as impersonal.*

B: Clare mentions induction but doesn't say that it should be comprehensive.

C: She does not mention colleagues interacting.

27 B: *if you frame the question like this, 'How can we do things differently?' he (the employee) feels involved and suggests possible solutions.*

A: James mentions an employee *going on the defensive* because a manager frames a question in a particular way, but he is not suggesting that all managers speak too forcibly.

C: Similarly, he does not suggest that all employees will be alarmed when speaking to managers.

28 B: *If the customer naturally speaks fast, I echo that. Research suggests that people are more receptive to information that's conveyed at their own rate.*

A: Clare says that she was told on a course to speak slowly and clearly, but then goes on to reject this advice.

C: Maintaining eye contact was also mentioned on a course, but Clare advises that *you shouldn't stare as that's unnerving.*

29 A: *errors in spelling are still inadmissible to my way of thinking. The golden rule is: do people the courtesy of proofreading your text.*

B: He suggests that things have changed and *notions of correctness have loosened up.*

C: He mentions *courtesy* but in the sense of being polite enough to check for mistakes rather than writing in a polite style.

30 C: *Don't overlook the ease with which we can cover the globe nowadays with long-haul flights, … it's made business trips so much more possible.*

A: She says face-to-face meetings are better than video conferencing.

B: She doesn't agree with the interviewer's suggestion that the computer has played the greatest role.

Further practice and guidance (p85)

A detailed study

1 1 She says *Emails flood into our inboxes* i.e. there are a lot of them. She also says *electronic messages are unparalleled (excellent) for conveying facts fast.*

2 No, she just doesn't think that they're good at expressing feelings.

3 She says *… emotion … comes through body language and tone of voice.* She means that you need to meet face to face with someone to express what you feel and understand their feelings.

4 Yes, she thinks they're essential – *without* (them) *co-operation on projects is jeopardized* (put at risk). Note that the words 'discussion' and 'face to face' are not said.

5 She says *Voicemails clog* (fill up) *our phones daily.*

6 No, she doesn't mention the sound quality.

2 1 James mentions option B – expressing clearly is *certainly an issue* and option A – *opportunity to find out where the other person's coming from.*

2 Clare mentions option A – *hearing them out first and then summarizing what they'd said* and option C – *repeating the management line.* So the answer to the question is option A because they both say it is important.

3 Clare signals that she shares James's view on listening carefully to other people's views when she says, *I couldn't agree more.* Although this phrase contains a negative verb, it is used to signal strong agreement.

4 Phrases to indicate agreement include

- *Absolutely / Exactly / Right*
- *No problem*
- *I think that would be best*
- *I couldn't agree more*

Phrases to indicate disagreement include

- *I see what you mean,* **but** *… / I take your point* **but** *…*
- *Up to a point* **but** *…*
- *That's true,* **but**…
- *That might be a problem,* **though**
- *Are you sure that's wise?*

Note that disagreement is often expressed in a more tentative way than agreement, in order not to give offence.

p88 SPEAKING Part Three

Further practice and guidance (p89)

A detailed study
Agreeing and disagreeing

1 b (disagree)

2 a (agree)

3 a (disagree)

4 b (agree)

5 a (agree)

6 a (disagree)

TEST 4

p90–91 READING Part One

Questions 1–8

0 B: *Its staff retention rate is also very good, with 80 per cent staying for more than a year.*

1 C: *The range offered by John Lewis protects it from falls in certain sectors.*

2 A: *And crucially, they were given joint ownership of the company.*

3 D: *In fact, it could be the case that the company is best equipped to deal with falling consumer spending. The people who will still have disposable income burning a hole in their well-tailored pockets will be those in professional jobs. In other words, just the sort of people you might meet in John Lewis.*

4 E: *It succeeds not because of its philosophy, but owing to its very successful online operation.*

5 B: *it's hard not to reach the conclusion that motivated staff have a pretty big impact on a company's performance* and *And if you ask John Lewis customers, they are often fulsome in their praise of the staff.*

6 A: *That's why they reap a slice of the profits each year.*

7 E: *Its success is more down to latching on to a growing upper-middle class customer base than any "radical" philosophy.*

8 C: *and locating stores in pockets where they know they will find their customer base.*

p92–93 READING Part Two

Questions 9–14

0 H: *The greater part of their income comes from the sale of manufactured goods. These cover anything from garden furniture, fountains and wooden decking to wind chimes, aquariums and patio heaters.*

their refers to the garden centres in the previous sentence. The previous sentence has mentioned the income of the centres (£2 billion) and this expands on that point. The sentence after the gap talks about *restaurants and shops* i.e. elaborating further on other sources of income outlined in the gapped sentence.

9 C: *Having demonstrated that they can diversify into other, more lucrative, areas, you would think that all is rosy in the garden centre world.*

they refers to the centres mentioned in the previous sentences; *diversify* refers to the other sources of income mentioned previously and in the previous sentence. *Not quite* in the sentence after the gap refutes a proposition – this is in the final clause (*you would think* ...) in the gapped sentence.

10 G: *Besides obvious rivals such as the Do-It-Yourself stores, supermarkets have declared plans to take a "significant" share of the garden market in plants.*

rivals gives a reason for the slowdown mentioned in the previous sentence; in the sentence after the gap *also face stiff competition* refers back to previously mentioned competition.

11 E: *Briercliffe points to the way in which Dutch growers have all co-operated to ensure that the whole process from planting to shop delivery is highly mechanised and that as a result they can offer the most competitive prices.*

points to the way in which means that this is an example of something mentioned previously i.e. *stiff competition*. *Dutch growers* refers to the *market in The Netherlands* mentioned in the previous sentence. Also *answer* in the sentence after the gap refers back to the problem posed by Dutch growers in the gapped sentence.

12 A: *By adopting such techniques for their own businesses, argues the HTA, garden centres will be better equipped to deal with the competition, as well as being more efficiently run operations in their own right.*

such techniques refers back to the concept of lean management mentioned in the previous sentence.

13 D: *The argument is that 95 per cent of actions in most companies, such as delays, movement, excess production and searching for things, are non-value adding.*

95 per cent of actions is the rest of the percentage for *5 per cent of actions* in the sentence which follows the gap. The sentence after the gap also explains what value-adding is as opposed to *non-value adding* mentioned here.

14 F: *In the case of Chessington Garden Centre, which started out growing budded roses and potatoes and selling eggs, this means it now makes an annual profit of more than £5m.*

In the case of shows that this sentence is an example of what has gone before i.e. an example of the success of lean management techniques described in the previous two sentences. The phrase *this means* refers back to the lean philosophy mentioned in the previous sentence. In the sentence after the gap *the directors* refers to the directors of the centre mentioned in the gapped sentence.

Choice B: *The first day is dedicated to theory, while the second is about mapping processes within the business and day three is for implementing an action plan.*

There is no place in the text where this sentence would fit.

p94–95 READING Part Three

Questions 15–20

15 B: *But all sales training is based on replicating successful behaviour, things that worked for other people in the past.* (line 2)

A: The text says that people's favourite sales are smooth and easy but not that selling generally is straightforward.

C: The text says that time is important but not that sales can be achieved in a limited time.

D: The text says not to waste time on people who can't decide.

16 C: *It's unlikely that your first sale was a fluke, to the only dentist in the world who needs what you do; more likely there are other dentists around with similar challenges.* (line 11)

A: Vertical markets are markets that are aligned to your original sales; the example of the dentist talks about selling to other dentists i.e. the same market.

B: Again 'wide' refers to the breadth of the market, not the number of people in one market.

D: The text talks about using the first sale you make, not the importance of a single sale.

17 A: *… encourage them to spread the word in their local community of dentists, and particularly when they head off to a trade show or convention.* (line 16)

B: The text does not talk about paying people.

C: The text explains you are lucky if your first sale is to an expert but not that you should ensure this.

D: The text talks about other people benefiting financially from recommendations, not whether or not you pay people.

18 B: *A good start is to find the 'tiniest thing' you can do for them. This is a good way to prove quickly what you do* (line 24)

A: The text talks about what you do but not how hard you may or may not work.

C: The text refers to eliminating people who can't make quick decisions but not that this is a reason.

D: The text does not mention whether or not sales will increase and does not connect quiet times with your effort or increased sales.

19 D: *trying too hard can have the opposite effect* (line 30)

A: The text talks about referrals but not in the context of you trying hard.

B: The text says sales may depend on quality but not in relation to you trying to do anything.

C: The text talks about everyone else telling their friends, not you.

20 C: *Everyone likes to deal with someone who is 'just around the corner'* (line 34); *dealing with the occasional problems swiftly and fairly.* (line 37); *'nice' is about being easy to deal with* (line 37)

A: The text says you will get sales in your local area but does not mention 'best' sales.

B: The text does not compare the three qualities but mentions them all equally. *Only* (line 35) means *simply* here.

D: The text talks about how to deal with or treat people but does not mention consistency.

p98–99 READING Part Four

Questions 21–30

0 **A:** *gaps* = from the expression 'gaps in the market'– niches which other companies have not exploited; *space* is used for physical room e.g. a space for another filing cabinet in the office; *hole* means a hollow place; *blank* means a space which is not written on – a blank piece of paper in a document.

21 **D:** *rival* = stand in an equally strong position or in nearly as strong a position as another company; *pressure* = apply physical force to something; *compare* = make a comparison with something; *compete* means to be in the same field of business and trying to attract the same customers, but not necessarily in an equal position to the other company.

22 **C:** *buyouts* = a management buyout means the purchase of a company by its own managers; *purchases* is a more general word for buying goods; *mergers* happen when two companies combine; *takeovers* occur when one company assumes control of another one.

23 **A:** *overhead* = an expense, something which is not making a profit; *outflow* is an outward current e.g. waste water that is leaving a factory; *outcome* is a result of a procedure; *overload* is an excessive load on, for example, a lorry or an electrical system.

24 **B:** *core* = often used with *activity* to mean the main business of a company; *critical* means serious, e.g. a critical financial position; *chief* means head or first as in 'my chief concern is cutting costs'. It would not collocate with 'activity'; *essential* means necessary.

25 **C:** *ancillary activities* = subordinate activities in a business; *substitute* = something or someone that is used in place of the original; *extra* = more than usual, or more than necessary, for example, employ extra staff at busy periods; *accessory* = contributing and is often used to mean assisting in a crime.

26 **D:** *enhance* = a verb that is often used in business to mean to raise in value or quality; *intensify* = to make more concentrated; *heighten* is often used with emotions, to make them stronger; *reinforce* = strengthen physically e.g. reinforced concrete (concrete strengthened by the addition of steel bars).

27 **C:** *outsourcing* = contracting work/ services to an outside supplier; *outputting* means sending out or producing, for example, data; *offloading* means getting rid of unwanted goods, possibly at very low prices; *offsetting* means to put one thing against another e.g. the cost of equipment can be offset against tax.

28 **D:** *providing* = to supply and is often used with a service; *creating* means inventing something new and takes the preposition 'for', not 'to'; *tendering* means making a formal offer or a bid for a contract; *producing* is used for making goods.

29 **B:** *sector* = a division of a market and is also used in 'public/private sector'; *segment* means *a part of* e.g. a circle that has been cut off by a straight line; *portion* is often used in the catering trade to mean the amount of food that is served to one person; *department* is a section of an organisation, for example the Finance Department.

30 **A:** *transactions* = deals that are negotiated in business or when individuals buy and sell goods and property; *trades* can mean deals but would not collocate with *property*; *trade* is more often used in the singular to indicate people in a particular occupation e.g. the book trade, or as a verb e.g. to trade in shares on the stock market; *promotions* mean advertising goods or services; *undertakings* in business terms are projects that a company engages in.

p100 READING Part Five

Questions 31–40

 0 AGO: missing time adverb indicating past

31 BY: missing preposition after passive verb

32 THEIR: missing pronoun, plural to accord with 'organisations'

33 FROM: missing preposition of movement 'from…to'

34 AS: missing conjunction in fixed phrase 'as a consequence/as a result'

35 TOWARDS/FOR: missing preposition, meaning *in the direction of*

36 ALTHOUGH/THOUGH/WHILE/WHILST: missing conjunction meaning *in spite of the fact that*

37 PART: missing noun in fixed phrase 'feel part of ' – feel they belong to a group

38 AND: missing conjunction often used at the end of a list of things or ideas

39 SUCH: missing adjective meaning 'so', used in the construction *such* + noun + *that*

40 WITHOUT: missing negative preposition meaning 'not having'. The word 'difficult' suggests that a negative word is needed.

p101 READING Part Six

Questions 41–52

 0 CORRECT

00 AND: An adjective does not need to be joined to a compound noun by 'and'.

41 CORRECT

42 AS: 'According to' means 'on the authority of' and does not need 'as'.

43 WHICH: Past participles like 'based' can follow directly after the verb. If a relative pronoun is used, it is followed by a clause – 'which are based in the south-east'.

44 CORRECT

45 CORRECT

46 MORE: indicates the first element of a comparison but that is already in place in 'a greater threat'.

47 MOST: precedes a superlative but there is no superlative here.

48 EITHER: introduces the first of two or more alternatives, but there is only one reason stated here – lack of staff.

49 ALTHOUGH: is followed or preceded by a contrasting statement. There is no contrast here.

50 CORRECT

51 THE: The definite article is not used when talking or writing in general terms – see 'stereotypical adverts' which has no article.

52 BY: The 'ing' form of the verb is the subject of the clause and so does not need the agent preposition 'by'.

Further practice and guidance (p102)

Preparation strategies

1 This will benefit Part Five most, since some of the questions are aimed at the type of mistakes that students often make. It will also help you with Part Six, since that involves proof reading for errors.

2 This strategy will help particularly with Part Four because this tests your vocabulary, collocations, fixed phrases etc. Reading widely will help with every aspect of the test as it is the best way not only to widen your vocabulary, but also to get a sense of style and register and of the way sentences are put together.

3 This will help you particularly with Part Six, since this is a proof reading task. Learning to check written work is a very valuable skill, which will prove useful in Business English and in professional life.

4 Collecting vocabulary and phrases in a lexical field is a good way to help you prepare for Part Four, but the focus on collocations and phrases will also help you with Parts Five and Six.

p103 WRITING Part One

Sample answer:

Generally sales of different types of holidays fluctuated across the year according to season. Unsurprisingly, ski holidays sold best in the first quarter peaking at 40,000. This then dipped dramatically in the second quarter, although a small number were still sold then. No ski holidays were sold in the third quarter but sales rose again in the fourth quarter exceeding sales in April-June. Beach holidays sold throughout the year peaking in the summer months at 50,000. However a significant number, 20,000, were sold in the first quarter with dips in the second and fourth quarter. City holidays sold more consistently throughout the year with the main peaks being in the second and fourth quarter. The best seasons for sales overall were the first and third quarter with substantially fewer holidays being sold in the second and fourth quarter.

(140 words)

The report:

- compares sales of the three different types of holidays

- has a summary sentence at the beginning

- discusses each holiday separately, which is less clumsy and repetitive than comparing each quarter.

p104 WRITING Part Two

Question 4: the proposal

Sample answer:

Purpose

The aim of this proposal is to make suggestions about improving the training service for staff.

Problems with the External Training Service

The problem with the external training service is that its trainers are not as good as they could be. Although some of them have considerable experience, others do not. They also tend to run generic courses which are not specifically tailored to our needs. We do need some generic training but we also need some specifically targeted training.

Advantages of in-house training

The advantages of in-house training are not just that we could tailor the training more precisely to the needs of staff and the company but also that it would save money. Although we may have to employ trainers, we could also use current staff and we would not be paying overheads. The training programme could be adapted as it goes along so would be constantly evolving with our needs.

How an in-house training programme could be organised

My suggestion is that we identify people within the company who have specific skills that they can usefully pass on. We could then give them some help in how to run training sessions. We could also employ two or three professional trainers full-time to run a training department.

Recommendation

Given the problems with the current training service I would strongly recommend that we explore the possibility of setting up an in-house training service both to provide the precise training staff need and to cut costs.

(248 words)

The sample proposal:

- addresses the three content points in the question (see headings)

- uses appropriately formal language, e.g. Given the problems with the current training service I would strongly recommend …

- is organized appropriately, e.g. with paragraphing and headings

- would inform the target reader effectively

Further practice and guidance (p105–106)

A detailed study

1 **2 or 4:** A proposal is usually written for someone above you in the company who wants your ideas or suggestions about something or it may be for someone at the same level as you but, for example, working in a different department.

2 Report & proposal: 1, 2, 3, 4, 6, 8

Report only: 5

Proposal only: 7, 9

4 **1a** the first heading should reflect the aim or purpose

2b Personal pronouns should not be included in headings; *problems* is more objective than *dissatisfied* (which reflects an emotional response)

3b Personal pronouns should not be included in headings; the heading should indicate that the advantages are objective not personal, e.g. *advantages of* not *why I think*

4a *The ways we could have* is very vague; **a** uses more precise language

5b *Conclusion* is more appropriate for a report after an evaluation (i.e. the conclusion of your evaluation). *Recommendation* is the main focus of a proposal.

5 (suggested answers)

1 Feedback from staff indicated there was some dissatisfaction with the training.

2 All the staff in the department were interviewed and complaints were made about the programme.

3 Staff in the IT department could be used to train others in IT systems.

4 It was suggested by the Head of HR that training sessions could be run during the lunch hours.

5 In my view, it would be worth investigating the possibility of employing trainers within the company.

6

The problem with the external training service is that its trainers are not as good as they could be. Although some of them have considerable experience, others do not. They also tend to run generic courses which are not specifically tailored to our needs. We need some generic training such as: health and safety, basic IT skills, etc. but we also need some specifically targeted training, which could probably best be delivered by people who work in-house and know the company well.

My suggestion is that we identify people within the company who have specific skills that they can usefully pass on. We could then give them some help in how to run training sessions.

p107 LISTENING Part One

Questions 1–12

1 *(company) absence records: This first became apparent when the company absence records were analysed as part of an annual review.*

2 *exit interviews: HR people held exit interviews too, when employees were moving on from the company.*

The answer is not 'questionnaires' as employees completed these themselves in their departments. The question mentions 'Personnel', which matches HR in the recording.

3 *(trades) union representatives/reps: talking casually to people across the staffing levels, including union representatives and management.*

4 *steering group: it was decided to set up a steering group, which I led as Head of the Health and Safety unit.*

5 *counselling service: few people were aware of our counselling service, which is available to all staff.*

6 *primary plan: Finally, after lengthy consultation, a primary plan was drawn up.*

7 *responsibility: everyone in the company bore a responsibility for coping with stress.*

8 *risk assessment tool: providing them with what we called 'a risk assessment tool', enabling them to identify potential causes of stress.*

Note that the ' ' round the gap in this question indicate that the answer is a proper name or title, and that the full name is required.

9 **control measures:** *the trainers demonstrated the range of what they referred to as 'control measures' and helped managers decide which would work best.*

The phrase 'what they referred to as' in the recording matches 'so-called' in the question. This is another way of indicating that a name is required. In this case writing 'measures' alone would not be sufficient.

10 **prevention:** *the trainers explained that the main emphasis was on prevention.*

11 **case studies:** *... working through case studies together. Managers found these last particularly useful in identifying steps they could take in their departments.*

The answer is not 'input sessions' as managers had to listen to those.

12 **£255,000 / 255,000 pounds:** *days lost to stress had come down from their peak by over 70%, which is an amazing achievement. That equates to a saving of £255,000.*

The answer is not 70%, because the question says 'a total of ' which indicates a sum of money. The other figure that is mentioned – £147,000 – is not right either, because this is the total expenditure on training, not the money saved on absences.

There will occasionally be answers in the form of numbers in this part of the Listening test. You will need to listen carefully, because there will be other numbers as distraction.

p108 LISTENING Part Two

Questions 13–22

13 **H:** *Someone suggested that sales staff could be encouraged to imagine how they'd feel if they were purchasing goods from us – how they'd prefer to be treated.*

14 **C:** *considerable thought had gone into ensuring that all employees were well up on the features of the different items in our product range.*

15 **F:** *failing to understand what people in the service department said when describing what was wrong with your car. ... staff training which focused on the avoidance of specialist terminology when talking to customers.*

16 **D:** *a new system to try to adapt to customers' requirements, like getting something very quickly or visiting people after hours.*

17 **B:** *our drive to improve customer care and focus on calling clients after they'd signed up for a contract to check whether it was providing the assistance and security they wanted.*

18 **C:** *After six months it was clear that the balance sheet looked much healthier.*

19 **D:** *One index that had risen quite dramatically was the one that shows the proportion of repeat business that the company had gained.*

20 **A:** *Our employees said they found interacting with the customers much more fulfilling.*

21 **G:** *our business has a different culture – it's able to react faster to changing circumstances and that should stand us in good stead in future.*

22 **H:** *our service contracts were more tailored to their needs than in the past.*

p109–110 LISTENING Part Three

23 **A:** *(Money) seems less of an issue though as they go up the ladder* (i.e. get promoted)

B: Mark mentions living costs like setting up home, but he does not talk about them increasing.

C: Mark talks about perks (benefits) but does not say that they have to be valuable ones.

24 **B:** *a sense of being part of, not just the unit you work in, but the company as a whole. That's something you wouldn't give up lightly.*

A: Pam doesn't mention the people you work with.

C: Mark is the one who mentions a sunny workspace with a nice view. Pam says that would be nice, but it isn't the key point.

25 **B:** *it was about knowing that what you contributed was appreciated.... getting the odd word or a pat on the back from her line manager and colleagues when something had gone well.*

A: Mark mentions award ceremonies, but suggests these are not what motivate people

C: He also mentions big prizes like holidays in California, but does not suggest this raises competitiveness.

26 C: *Mark: I've heard it said that people don't join a company because the managers are good, but they certainly leave because of bad ones.*

Pam: That's not a cheering thought, is it, but I'm sure we've all been there.

A: Mark says managers are overworked but Pam doesn't.

B: Pam mentions the effects of team-building courses but Mark rejects this.

27 A: *But there are other things, like being able to plan your core time to avoid the rush hour or collect the kids.*

B: He mentions going travelling for six months but suggests that's of limited appeal.

C: Pam mentions working from home, not Mark.

28 C: *If a company can provide counselling and suggest what route they could take over the years, that might be the deciding factor.*

A: She mentions expensive tuition but doesn't say that staff would expect the company to pay for it.

B: She says people welcome free time initially after completing their qualifications, but suggests that's not so much of an issue later on.

29 B: *providing new stimuli by offering sideways moves or additional responsibilities may be one solution.*

A: He mentions 'repetitiveness' but does not suggest that people get careless.

C: He talks about people feeling secure, 'which often suits an organisation', so there is no suggestion that companies want to dismiss these people.

30 A: *I was just wondering about appointing senior managers for an agreed time, say three years.*

B: Mark suggests rotating posts but Pam rejects that as potentially confusing.

C: She talks about handing good people to the competition, but she does not mean secondment, she means they leave because there is no chance of promotion.

Further practice and guidance (p111–112)

Exam information

1 Part Two. However, if you leave Task Two to the second listening, you will only have one opportunity to find the answer. It would be better to attempt both tasks in the first listening, if you can.

2 Part One

3 Part One. You must write in pencil and in capital letters on the answer sheet.

4 Part Three. See the Further Practice section in Test Three (page 85)

5 All three parts. The instructions remind you of what you have to do and also set the context for the listening, for example: *You will hear a manager talking to his team about a training seminar.*

6 All three parts. It is always worth writing something. If you leave a question blank you will get no marks. If you write something, you might just be right. No marks are subtracted for wrong answers.

A detailed study

Part One

1 Perso**nnel** department or Human Resources (Perso**nal** means 'relating to a person')

2 princi**ple** or main, most important (princi**pal** means the Head, e.g. the Principal of the college)

3 station**ery** includes paper, pens, envelopes, labels etc. (station**ary** means not moving e.g. a stationary vehicle)

4 bank**rupt**/bank**ruptcy**

5 competenc**ies** –words with a consonant (b, c, d, etc) before a final 'y' are spelt 'ies' in the plural e.g. 'tries'. Words with a vowel (a, e, i, o, u) before a final 'y' are spelt 'ys' in the plural e.g. 'buys'.

6 se**cretarial**/se**cret**ary

7 a**ccommo**dation/a**ccommo**date

8 a**pp**raisal/a**pp**raise

9 copy**right** (*right* means entitlement)

10 ineffici**en**cy/ineffici**ent**/suffici**ent**

Part Two

1 Task One focuses on 'the customer relations strategy each person adopted'.

2 The focus is on a past action: 'each person adopt**ed**'

3 Task Two focuses on 'the main benefit that has been gained by a focus on customer relations'.

4 The focus is on the past: 'has been gained'.

5 The two key words are 'main benefit' If the speaker mentions several benefits, you must choose the one he or she identifies as the most important one.

6 The two sentences are: 'Someone suggested that sales staff could be encouraged to imagine how they'd feel if they were purchasing goods from us – how they'd prefer to be treated. We **decided to try that** and it made a difference'.

7 It is option H – try to see the company from the customer's point of view.

8 The distractors are: 'brochures' and 'customer response questionnaires' – options A and G.

9 The phrase 'so those were put on one side' makes A and G impossible as answers, because they were not the strategies that the speaker adopted.

10 The answer is 'the balance sheet looked much healthier'.

11 The distractor is 'advertising budget … to be lower – option B.

12 The phrase 'time will tell on that one' rules option B out, because it is clearly not a 'main' benefit, as its effects haven't been achieved yet.

p113–115 SPEAKING

Further practice and guidance (p116–117)

Exam Tips

Part One

Suggested responses:

1 … management skills, for example team building and motivation.

2 … because I think it would be much more rewarding than working for a big company.

3 … in order to make enough money to give their family a good lifestyle.

Part Two

1 b

2 e

3 d

4 c

5 a

Possible questions on your partner's mini-presentation:

1 How important is a pleasant work environment in persuading staff to stay?

2 What role does salary play in retaining staff?

Part Three

1 c: … it is a question of checking carefully whether a particular trade fair is in an appropriate place and is likely to attract the right sort of visitors to your stand.

2 d: … look out for potential customers at all times and make sure they have all the information they need.

3 a: … of the company and encourage potential clients to get in contact.

4 b: … products or services the public want and get feedback about what competitors are offering.

Listening scripts

TEST 1

Part 1 Questions 1–12

One of the most exciting but potentially most challenging tasks you'll face is to manage a project. Even if it's quite a small one, success will stand you in good stead in future. I think successful projects depend largely on setting up effective systems so I'd like to give you some tips now.

However small the project, it's essential to get your superior's approval for what you're planning, that means initially for what are referred to as the 'terms of reference'. These need careful thought so don't try to rush this phase. It often requires several drafts before you get everything right. It's worth it though, as it may well save you time in the long run.

While we're thinking about time, don't be too ambitious with the timescale. Projects frequently come in late. Also, one thing you'll need to establish is a series of 'break points' during the project so you'll be able to monitor progress at fixed times.

Another thing, it's best to choose your team as soon as possible. This allows members to acquire ownership of the project and start thinking how their contribution can best be made.

Once you've taken these key initial steps, you can focus on the detail. One way you can oversee the different components is to put together a 'Critical Path Analysis'. This can be done on computer. The program will indicate in what order you should do the different assignments and you can then track them against a timeline. It's quite easy to set up. Another thing, finances need to be planned carefully too and scheduled. One issue that can cause problems, for example, is if suppliers withhold goods because their invoices haven't been paid!

You may think that good planning should mean there won't be any complications. But it's likely that there will be, so you should set up a contingency budget. This will allow you to allocate funds to cope with any unforeseen issue when it occurs.

Now let's think about managing the team. Ideally, you've selected good people, but they may not all be very experienced. In any event, providing each one with a written outline which indicates their role in the project will save headaches later. One of the most difficult things is deciding how much you can hand over without interfering. Some innovative people lose impetus if the manager's always checking up on them. They need complete freedom, while inexperienced staff want less – in fact they like their boss to be involved in their day-to-day decisions. So try to evaluate each person's needs and preferred working style. Keeping the team motivated is equally important. All staff need praise. This oils the wheels and helps morale even more than money does.

As I've said, you need to check on developments at prearranged intervals. You shouldn't keep the results to yourself, though. Some managers keep in contact with their team by email. That's fine for everyday stuff, but important news needs to be given face-to-face. So call them all in and use the opportunity to discuss the next steps. That brings me to another point, which I should have made earlier. All this checking that you're doing should be documented properly. If something goes wrong, you'll need to analyse why it happened. So keep careful records of everything.

Finally, let's think about the end of the project, which will hopefully arrive on time and on budget. This is the moment to hold a review meeting with the team to reflect on your successes and learn from any mistakes, so that you can do even better next time around.

Part 2   Questions 13–17

Speaker 1

I go to lots of meetings in this job – too many really. People spend hours analysing what's happened at department or company level – most of which you know already, and anyway everything's in the past so you can't change it! That sounds rather critical, but some meetings are more constructive, like the one last week. The objective was to settle what to attempt in the next twelve months and agree who should undertake which elements. There was a lot of discussion from everyone – very amicable on the whole. At the end the MD insisted on going through what we'd committed to and checking our understanding of our contributions. It took an extra half hour, though I felt this was worth replicating in future as it should avoid potential mix-ups.

Speaker 2

I've got a new line manager and I was dreading going to a meeting with him. Well, it's the end of the financial year, when the board review salaries and plan expenditure. It's also the period when we have our individual achievements and failures examined and receive feedback. I'm not against this in principle, it's just the way it's handled. My last boss used to arrive out of breath, shuffle through papers, which he was clearly looking at for the first time, and make some vague comments about my work, without allowing any interventions or explanations. This time, though, the new guy had made a comprehensive chart of my sales totals. So the meeting was clear and helpful and I left feeling positive. That's definitely the way to go.

Speaker 3

I'm not keen on all-day meetings at Head Office. There's lots to discuss so a full day's needed, but it's difficult to keep concentrating, especially in the afternoon! I managed to stay focused during the last one though. I decided that it was the way it had been organized – a number of short points which needed active participation straight after lunch, while the more complex stuff had been discussed fully first thing. I must remember to do that. These meetings where we analyse the pros and cons of possible additions to our range are very important. An added bonus is that we sometimes get a chance to see how junior staff are shaping up, because they occasionally give short presentations on the proposed models. That's really good practice for them.

Speaker 4

I was fed up last night. I'd been sitting all afternoon with five other people from the department trying to reach a decision. It wasn't easy so we did need time to assess the different choices. Finding the right person to appoint is tricky as you've got to consider how they'd fit in with the rest of the team and that's particularly important in a small operation like ours.

Anyway, that wasn't what irritated me. I really respect our Head of Department, but she's not a great chair. I can't fault the ground work she does before meetings or the documents she draws up. It's just that she isn't firm enough so one or two people tend to take over. I wouldn't allow that, because it can unbalance a meeting.

Speaker 5

We went to AER recently for a meeting which didn't go as well as we'd hoped unfortunately. Our aim for the day was to work out some more favourable conditions on the bid we'd put in to develop a large site for them. We didn't exactly come away empty-handed but we had to accept tighter deadlines than we'd like. Anyway, I suppose it was quite an instructive session for some of our guys on what to look out for in future. I blame AER's Manager actually. He kept allowing people to raise issues that had no bearing on the matter in hand and this made us lose focus, even though we kept bringing the discussion back to the main agenda. That really has to be avoided in my view.

Part 3　Questions 23–30

Int: I'm delighted to welcome Markus Neuman who's made a name as an internet business coach. Markus, was training always your aim?

Mar: Well, after completing an economics degree, I toyed with the idea of becoming a university tutor. But much as I valued my college life and the prospect of doing research, I felt I ought to experience the cut and thrust of the 'real world', and to me that meant share trading and the adrenalin rush of prices rising and falling. My father was an accountant so I'd always been around figures.

Int: And how did you feel about beginning your first job?

Mar: I started off wearing one of my dad's suits. He had good taste in clothes, my dad, so it was beautifully made, but he's thicker-set than me and it hung off me. I bought myself a new one with my first paycheck and that felt good. But looking back, I realise that the job was like that suit. I was too entrepreneurial to fit in somewhere where I had to take orders from people, particularly if I didn't respect them.

Int: You worked for several household names for ten years before making your move. Do you regret that time?

Mar: It was a hard grind, what with the incredibly long hours and the hugely cutthroat atmosphere, though that did give me a real buzz at times. It was also a steep learning curve, but I can't say it wasn't worth the effort. I wouldn't have got where I am now without it, that's for sure.

Int: So eventually you decided to set up on your own. How did that happen?

Mar: I was coming up to the big 3 0 – a time for reflection. I'd got all the material comforts and I could have stayed and made some serious money. Then I thought, 'Life's too short to toil away realising other people's dreams. It's time I followed my own.' I knew it would be risky, but I was getting stale – I'd absorbed everything there was to know – so I became an internet coach

Int: So what sets your company apart from the rest?

Mar: My main strand is helping self-employed people grow their businesses with the power of the internet, something that's hardly original now. What's different is that I've got a facility which I call a 'refuge', where entrepreneurs can come and explore different possibilities before starting up on their own. And I also do conference sessions on the stock variety of topics to keep up my contacts.

Int: Working with the internet must be challenging…

Mar: Absolutely! It's in such a state of flux. This whole social networking phenomenon, for example, didn't even exist a few years ago and now it's everywhere and it's not just for teenagers with time on their hands – it's crucial in the business world too. The web's just so vast now, that keeping abreast of the innovations is more than I can cope with. So I drafted in some fellow enthusiasts to share the load.

Int: You're obviously a self-motivator, so advising clients on setting relevant goals must be key in your work.

Mar: Goal setting has its place, certainly. You'd be amazed though, at the number of entrepreneurs who spend so long drafting the perfect business plan that they never get their venture off the ground! People would be so much better off focusing on what they're good at and what turns them on and then trying to combine these two things to see if their scheme has any legs. If they find there's interest in what they're offering, that's the moment to map out targets and create systems to implement them.

Int: Finally, Markus, in this electronic age where executives complain that technology, far from saving time, is making them contactable at any moment, and thus extending the working day, what words of wisdom would you pass on?

Mar: I spent years being paid handsomely, but working such long hours that I had no leisure to enjoy my earnings. It took me ages to grasp that time's the real currency, and making every second count's the key. Look out for something that makes you want to leap out of bed in the morning and then hopefully find ways to get paid well for doing it!

TEST 2

Part 1   Questions 1–12

We've decided who's coming to Eurotech in six weeks, so I thought we'd get everyone together. As some of you haven't been to a trade fair before, I'm going to go through things in considerable detail so you get an overview of the process from beginning to end. Apologies to people who've done this lots of times.

Right, I'm going to start by telling you how we prepare for the fair. First we have to try to attract enough visitors to the stand. It's a huge fair so people don't go round everything. One way to do this is to pay to have a piece about Magnum printed in what's called 'the event programme'. Personally, I'm not convinced that it's worth paying a huge amount to put an advert in the national or local press, but lots of companies do. Talking of money, we also work out a budget beforehand so we know how much we've got to work with. Exhibiting at these fairs doesn't come cheap. Then we have to decide what promotional merchandise we're going to take. These things aren't just free gifts for the casual visitor. You want your objects to remind customers about you. So you have to choose something that'll transmit an appropriate image of the company, and I think this glass paper weight will do that.

Let's move on to the fair itself. We'll get the stand set up the day before, arrange the display and check the projector's OK. We must remember to take a back-up for that, just in case it stops working, though. We'll all have our laptops anyway, won't we?

Now, in order to create a more professional feel we've had a special badge printed for each of you. So please keep that on at all times. Another thing, exhibition halls can be very airless places I find. We always have a rota so everyone gets breaks to prevent them falling asleep or getting too hungry, of course!

Now, when visitors come to the stand, introduce yourself and see if they have any queries. There'll be special notepads for you to write the contact details of potential customers and brochures to hand out. Most companies lay these out at the front of the stand. That looks good but a lot get wasted, so we'll display ours right at the back and only hand them out to potentially useful visitors. Remember to go through the main points with them and while you're doing that keep eye contact as that engages the visitor more. Give them your business card too, and if they're struggling with armfuls of other promotional material, you could offer a carrier bag. I've had some specially printed this year with the Magnum name, and that's also on some mineral water bottles. People might be grateful for one of those as it gets very hot in the hall.

Now, the fair lasts four days. What we do on the last evening after the doors close, is take down the stand, load up the van and then go back to the hotel. Then, before we go out for a good dinner, we have a debriefing just to assess what worked and what didn't, while everything's fresh in our minds. It's useful to measure how we did in relation to the targets we set months ago, you know, number of visitors, potential customers from different countries etcetera. Then, when we get back here and unpack, it'll be time to pursue all the leads we got. Depending on their potential, we'll phone, email or arrange a visit.

Now, any questions?

Part 2   Questions 13–17

Speaker 1

Sales declined last year so we decided to change the marketing mix. We held a brainstorming session and some people suggested sending out a mailshot in specific regions with a money-off coupon. That can have a very positive effect, though it tends to be short-term. Another more radical suggestion was to look at how the product range was presented, you know, colour of the wrapping, visuals, type of print and so on. After some thought we suggested that, and management agreed. Sales rose and, when we asked customers for their views, surprisingly, over 60% of respondents thought the sauces tasted different, and suspected we'd used real tomatoes instead of tomato flavouring. So what we'd intended to do, which was just create a younger more 'fun' image, had a different and much wider-reaching effect.

Speaker 2

We restyled one model in our range recently. What we tend to do on these occasions is send publicity out to existing and potential customers on our database. Postage is increasing though, so we wrote a factual piece instead, emphasising the new more eco-friendly aspects of the model and invited people from the national and specialist papers to headquarters to see it. We considered following up with an online promotion, but there are so many of those flashing up on screens at the moment. Anyway, we were pleased by the results. The timing could have been better, summer holidays had just started, but customer enquiries were good. We decided that something that appears in an article is considered more trustworthy than the best designed publicity material – human nature's fascinating!

Speaker 3

One of our recent ventures was quite successful. Marketing isn't an exact science and you do your best to research the market and release information on special deals in ways that consumers will find interesting and hopefully spend some time considering, although often we know things end up in the bin unread. Anyway, we went down an avenue we hadn't tried before and helped fund some local events. Obviously our name appeared on the programmes and in the venues. We didn't think much would come of it, and anyway it would be hard to analyse the response, but it was clear in the next few months that consumers of our services were considerably less mature, and reflected the general composition of the audiences at the events. It's definitely worth trying again.

Speaker 4

A new employee suggested an idea. I expected it to be internet-related – not that I'm against that. Lots of sales come through our website and our presence on web directories. No, her idea was that customers would buy more if they sat down and really examined what we offered carefully. When we tried out her proposal, sales did increase and a telephone survey revealed that was the reason. She believes people only glance at publicity offers sent by companies they use, however much they improve the way products are presented, because there's so much junk mail nowadays. However, if they receive a communication regularly, filled with information about changes in the firm and tips related to the products – in our case gardening hints – they'll pay attention, and it builds customer loyalty.

Speaker 5

We set ourselves the task last year of targeting a wider range of consumers. Our confectionery isn't cheap, nor is it that highly-priced, but customer surveys suggested that people thought of it as suitable for very special occasions rather than as a weekly treat, which is what we wanted them to think. The chocolates are well-presented in elegant silver packaging which might be helping to create this perception, I suppose. We'd placed advertising in various newspapers before, with limited success, so we tried something different – cardboard bins by the checkouts with small packets of chocolates and a picture of a group of friends watching TV – in other words a normal evening in. And it worked! Lots of new customers across the age range started to buy them, mainly at weekends.

Part 3   Questions 23–30

Woman: Frank, is now a good time to ask you about my MBA assignment?

Man: Sure, Julia. I need a break.

Woman: This module's 'Managing Change' – more specifically what can go wrong.

Man: An interesting area … Well, I think the biggest cause of failure is ….

Woman: trying to do things too quickly?…

Man: That's what coursebooks say and I'm sure it has a bearing. I think, though, where managers fall down is in believing that organizations themselves have to change, you know invent different systems, whereas it's really the people. If they don't trust the leadership or buy into the reason for change, it's a lost cause.

Woman: Right. And that leads on to something else, which is how you should prepare for change. I remember working in an office once when the boss suddenly announced enormous changes. Everyone was shocked.

Man: Did he explain the rationale behind them, like keeping up with competitors perhaps…?

Woman: He didn't, and that was part of the problem. We didn't feel involved.

Man: No, and that's alienating. Perhaps he was trying to save you from getting stressed….

Woman: Nice idea, though he was hardly the caring type. He probably underestimated our ability to grasp the situation.

Man: That raises another interesting point – the different ways people deal with change. Some are clearly more change-adept.

Woman: Presumably they're the really competent people who have everything under control.

Man: You'd think so, wouldn't you? Often though, those are precisely the people who cling to the established order. Staff who are happy to go with the flow tend to prove their worth in these changing situations.

Woman: I'd have thought it would be the highly creative people who'd be the most useful.

Man: As long as they don't mind if their ingenious new system has to go when the parameters alter again, but I'm afraid they do.

Woman: How does managing a big change, like transforming an organization, compare with managing incremental changes?

Man: Well, incremental change, improving performance and so on, is progressive and builds on past performance, which employees were part of. It's predictable too, while transformation isn't. Often what a company has been most successful at can act as an obstacle as it has to be abandoned in the redefining of what the company needs to become in future.

Woman: And that's painful for everyone concerned. I suppose communicating the need for change is crucial.

Man: Absolutely, and managers don't always get it right. They spend ages drafting speeches or articles for the company newsletter.

Woman: You mean the formal channels.

Man: Right. While the informal messages are overlooked, like the chats round the water cooler.

Woman: And people are becoming more sceptical now. Rhetoric flows over them and isn't accepted unless it's backed up by actions. Good point.

Man: It's always preferable to win people over if you can, rather than dragging them into anything. Here's a story I was told on my MBA. The North wind and the sun were competing to see who could strip a traveller of his coat. The wind blew very hard but the traveller wrapped the coat tighter round himself. Then the sun shone gently and the man took his coat off.

Woman: That's nice. I could use that in this piece of work.

Man: Good. Now, tell me what impresses you most about your course?

Woman: I'm enjoying the seminars. The tutors really know their stuff, as you'd expect, and they're quite approachable too. The contributions from my coursemates are absolutely first class

and that's really helpful in discussions. The materials too are tip-top, though some are a bit behind the times, but then the course has been running for years.

Man: I'm glad. It's hard doing an MBA and working full-time, so you need to feel it's worth it. Some people think it's the contacts you make on the course that'll be most useful in future.

Woman: You do meet really interesting people, though you might do that through work anyway. What makes it for me is being able to give space to working through theories and evaluating them for myself.

Man: You wouldn't think that'd be so valuable, would you, but it certainly is.

Woman: The facts that you learn in seminars and through reading are important too, though you can always pick those up for yourself later.

Man: I suppose so – if you're not lazy like me!

TEST 3

Part 1   Questions 1–12

Man:
Listen up everyone. Karen King has kindly agreed to lead a session on teambuilding as we prepare to set up teams to develop our new product range. So, without more ado, over to you, Karen.

Woman:
Good Morning everyone. I thought I'd start by outlining the key principles of successful teambuilding and then I'll answer questions.

So, what makes an effective team? In my view, it depends on working out initially what I call a 'shared vision' of the best way the team could operate. With this in place, commitment and motivation will follow. But this can't be achieved overnight. It takes time and seasoned leadership expertise to encourage the team to discuss the options fully and attain consensus on how to advance.

Another important task is to sort out the roles of the team members. There'll be a range of different talents and personalities which you must know how to use. Every team needs people to be innovative, but it also needs people who can focus on the details and spot any complications before they arise. People should be given scope to work to their strengths, but they'll also be expected to try to make up for whatever weakness arises in the team, since it's the performance of the whole that matters rather than individual achievements.

Having got the measure of your team, it's time to focus on what you have to deliver to the customers – in your case, a new product range. But you shouldn't only think about the external customers, there are others who are concerned in the outcome of your work, such as other departments, senior management, suppliers and so on. So check who these stakeholders are and what they expect of the team. Similarly, you must keep in mind the people who've commissioned the work you're undertaking and provided the resources for it. I like to call this group the 'sponsors', and you'll need to update them regularly on developments and let them know your ongoing requirements.

Remember to keep your focus on the members after the set-up phase. Personally, I find group activities help to create team spirit. I can see by the doubtful looks on your faces that you're not convinced! Certainly, things like weekends away or mountain climbing to help teams bond have received a bad press, and probably rightly so. But what I'm recommending is much less demanding. For example, you could organize a group lunch on Fridays. This would enable you to assess progress in an informal atmosphere. Things like this can help to foster a mood of trust between team members, something which will undoubtedly lead to greater efficiency.

I just want to warn you now of a few things to avoid. Teams are made up of people who don't always get on well. So be on the look out for any interpersonal issues. Deal with them quickly by talking things through with the individuals concerned, and, if necessary, change any work pairings to keep things smooth.

It's also important to establish early on that the team is not a place where a culture of blame can be tolerated. Lead the way on this one and own up at once to any mistake you make, rather than saying it was someone else's fault.

Finally, all workplaces are alive with gossip and this is an inevitable part of human interaction, I'm afraid. It can provide a bit of light relief round the water cooler, but it can

also be malicious and create divisions in a team, which you certainly don't want, so keep it to a minimum, if you can.

Part 2   Questions 13–22

Speaker One

I was giving a presentation at a fair in Chicago. I get nervous before speaking in unknown places, you know, will participants be able to see the stage or will my laptop work with the multimedia projector? In this case, though, I'd assisted my boss when he spoke there two years before, so I knew the hall was tip-top. What was making me uneasy, though, was the courier – the marketing brochures hadn't been delivered and I only had a few with me – but all was well in the end. I was hoping to make contacts and find out about a new machine tool company. No joy there, but someone from the *New York Times* came and he wrote a complimentary piece about our new range – a real bonus!

Speaker Two

I gave a short presentation recently to showcase everything we offer from the most basic of personal health insurance policies, up to the complex corporate ones. I'd designed some new materials, so I wasn't expecting much. It takes time to get used to new slides and learn how to exploit them properly, even when you're sure of your key points. Above all, I was uneasy about the people marketing had targeted with their mailshot – I wasn't convinced they'd focused on the right profile. To my surprise, though, everything went down very well, so well that the head of HR at Grants, you know, the international pharmaceutical company, contacted me later. We met and he's recommending our top-of-the-range policy to his board. My boss will be pleased if it works out!

Speaker Three

It's not easy to get your point across effectively. There are so many factors to consider, like crucially, how long to speak for. I've got that one sorted now though – I keep things brief. That way people's attention doesn't wander. I did get rather uptight last week because I wasn't convinced that I'd got the organisation of my talk right. I wanted to emphasise the positive benefits of my scheme, like potential cost savings in the components we buy in, and so I spent most of the time on that aspect. It could have appeared a bit one-sided. Fortunately, I seem to have judged it right. I was asked to say more about possible expansion and then, after some discussion in the group, my recommendation was accepted. What a relief!

Speaker Four

I gave a talk on stress management recently at a conference. It's hard to know which events are worth speaking at, but this one's proved useful over the years. It did so again this year. After my session, someone who works for a company with a series of upmarket hotels came up. She wanted to talk about the possibility of us running some sessions for their junior managers, focusing on customer relations and better communications. That's all fixed now and it should be worthwhile. Funny, when I remember the state I was getting into about my talk. I'd chosen a more artistic font for my slides and I was convinced things wouldn't be legible from the back. A change for me – it's usually the technology that worries me most.

Speaker Five

I was in two minds whether to go to Australia recently for a congress, set up by a new international architects association. The keynote speech and the topics sounded stimulating but you have to weigh up whether these events are worth the costs in terms of travel, accommodation and time too. I wasn't at all convinced. Anyway, I'm glad I went. My presentation on some recent projects our company has been involved in went well. Afterwards I talked to someone in the audience who worked for a newspaper group. The group want to relocate into a state-of-the-art building and he suggested we put in a bid to design it. And I'd thought the best we could hope for was to be asked to join the speakers' panel next year!

Part 3   Questions 23–30

Woman 1: I'm delighted to welcome Clare Swinbrook, CEO of Aldis Plastics and James Kilbride, Professor of Business Administration at Westland University. Our topic is better communication. When I was preparing I thought we might run

out of conversation since this is an age of excellent communication, thanks to technology. Am I right, Clare?

Woman 2: I can see why you'd think that. Emails flood into our inboxes, voicemails clog our phones daily. Don't get me wrong – electronic messages are unparalleled for conveying facts fast. The same isn't true though of emotion. That comes through body language and tone of voice, and without it, co-operation on projects, for example, is jeopardised in my view.

Woman 1: Are you a believer in meetings, James?

Man: Yes, providing they're handled properly. So many business people don't know how to do it.

Woman 1: Where do they go wrong? Don't they express themselves clearly enough?

Man: That's certainly an issue in some cases, but I think we need to go deeper. Many people consider meetings as a chance to get their point across, come what may. They fail to see that it's an opportunity to find out where the other person's coming from and then act accordingly.

Woman 2: I couldn't agree more. Take a meeting I had with trades union representatives. They had grievances and the atmosphere was tense. By hearing them out first and then summarising what they'd said, I managed to defuse the situation and move on. Repeating the management line, however firmly I'd stated it, wouldn't have worked.

Woman 1: What about regular internal meetings? Couldn't the facts be transmitted equally well on memos?

Man: I'm sure they could, but that's only part of it. People discuss issues at meetings. They can defend their views, even if they're not going to be acted on. What's more, this makes them feel they belong to the group and I think that's crucial to the successful working of a unit and indirectly to the organisation.

Woman 2: You mentioned memos a moment ago. That reminds me – people tend to have a preferred method of communication, whether it's memo, email or phone. Someone joining our company alienated his colleagues by always sending memos, which were seen as impersonal. So now, part of our induction includes tips on the preferred 'communication code', a bit like advising staff on dress code, if you like.

Woman 1: James. You've researched the language of business. Can you give us an example where language can influence an outcome?

Man: OK… Imagine you're a manager trying to find out about a procedure. If you ask closed questions, like 'Do you do it this way?', you'll only get a Yes/No answer. So you ask a supplementary question beginning with 'why' and the employee goes on the defensive and thinks he's being criticised. But if you frame the question like this, 'How can we do things differently?' he feels involved and suggests possible solutions. It does take practice, however, to self-edit.

Woman 1: Fascinating! Now, what about external communication, Clare?

Woman 2: When I was doing a sales course, they suggested that when trying to convince a potential customer you must talk slowly and clearly, maintaining eye contact continually. The eyes are certainly important, although you shouldn't stare as that's unnerving, but the speed can vary. If the customer naturally speaks fast, I echo that. Research suggests that people are more receptive to information that's conveyed at their own rate. Quite demanding at first but you get used to adapting!

Woman 1: We haven't mentioned good writing style. What's the key, James?

Man: Now that email's on the scene, things have changed. The old formal letter structure still applies in certain circumstances of course, but notions of correctness have loosened up,

though errors in spelling are still inadmissible to my way of thinking. The golden rule is: do people the courtesy of proofreading your text, whether it's an internal email or a client letter.

Woman 1: One last question. Don't you think the computer has played the greatest role in improving communication?

Woman 2: Most people would agree with you. Don't overlook the ease with which we can cover the globe nowadays with long-haul flights, though. I know that sounds odd but it's made business trips so much more possible, and discussing round a table beats video conferencing any day in my book.

TEST 4

Part 1   Questions 1–12

Good morning. My name's George Crump and I'm here to talk about how my company, Martins Finance, implemented a stress management solution. Martins has been a major player in the financial sector for over 100 years. Recently though, along with many financial companies, Martins has been through a process of rationalisation which has involved reducing the workforce considerably. This inevitably caused anxiety and the necessary changes in workload led to increased levels of stress. This first became apparent when the company absence records were analysed as part of an annual review two years ago, and levels were found to be much higher than normal.

Management decided to mount a full investigation. To do this we used a range of sources, starting with the most obvious – staff surveys. This involved employees completing anonymous questionnaires in their departments. HR people held exit interviews too, when employees were moving on from the company. Finally, we sampled as many reactions as we could by talking casually to people across the staffing levels, including union representatives and management.

But how to deal with this information? Our normal systems didn't seem appropriate, so it was decided to set up a steering group, which I led as Head of the Health and Safety unit. Our analysis showed that there wasn't **one** main cause of stress, but several causes and, not surprisingly, work demands and concerns about change featured highly. It was also clear that information on existing support systems was not getting through. For example, few people were aware of our counselling service, which is available to all staff.

The next thing was to work out what to do. We saw managing stress as a company-wide initiative of the same importance as dealing with other workplace hazards, such as fire. Finally, after lengthy consultation, a primary plan was drawn up. We all know that written procedures alone are pointless unless they're implemented company-wide, so we decided to introduce stress management training for all managers. The key was to make them aware that **everyone** in the company bore a responsibility for coping with stress.

The aim of the training was to empower managers, by providing them with what we called 'a risk assessment tool', enabling them to identify potential causes of stress. In the second phase, the trainers demonstrated the range of what they referred to as 'control measures' and helped managers decide which would work best in dealing with the problem. This didn't mean that a whole new set of procedures would be needed, as most of them were based on good management practice.

I imagine you're wondering how the training was received. I can't say that all our managers were thrilled at the idea! Some were distinctly sceptical. However, once the trainers explained that the main emphasis was on prevention, and they were given the figures of stress-related time-off, most saw the sense in it. The course involved listening to input sessions and working through case studies together. Managers found these last particularly useful in identifying steps they could take in their departments.

The training was only the start of a long-term commitment to addressing the problems of stress and so we weren't expecting any immediate improvement. However, a year from completing the roll-out, statistics showed that days lost to stress had come down from their peak by over 70%, which is an amazing achievement. That equates to a saving of £255,000 in lost wages. Considering that the expenditure on the training came to about £147,000, it's been a worthwhile investment and

the effects should continue to be felt for years.

Now, any questions?

Part 2   Questions 13–22

Speaker 1

We trade in a competitive area, so we decided to try to give our company a bit of an edge by focusing on customer relations. We brainstormed some options and then analysed how viable they were. Some important items like the brochures and customer response questionnaires had recently been revised so those were put on one side. Someone suggested that sales staff could be encouraged to imagine how they'd feel if they were purchasing goods from us – how they'd prefer to be treated. We decided to try that and it made a difference. After six months it was clear that the balance sheet looked much healthier. We also expect our advertising budget next year to be lower than in previous years, but time will tell on that one.

Speaker 2

We've been analyzing the company's performance over the last twelve months, checking statistics on, for example, market share and product placement. One index that had risen quite dramatically was the one that shows the proportion of repeat business that the company had gained. We tried to work out why that should be and looked at our customer systems and after-service care procedures. Very few adaptations had been made there during the year, though considerable thought had gone into ensuring that all employees were well up on the features of the different items in our product range. We came to the conclusion that customers had found that particularly helpful as the number of different models on offer today can be very confusing. So that was time and energy well spent.

Speaker 3

Good customer relations can be the factor that raises a company's standing, but finding different ways to improve them isn't easy. We did some research with our existing vehicle customers to discover what annoyed them. Various points emerged, including incomprehensible instruction manuals and failing to understand what people in the service department said when describing what was wrong with your car. We commissioned some staff training which focused on the avoidance of specialist terminology when talking to customers – after all, every business has its own jargon and car dealers are no exception. Customer surveys show that our efforts are possibly beginning to pay off. Our employees said they found interacting with the customers much more fulfilling, and that's crucial, as I think it'll translate into significant financial gains in time.

Speaker 4

If you read companies' mission statements and sales literature they all claim that customer service comes first. However, when you're a customer you find that some companies have rigid rules and procedures and very uncooperative staff who won't adapt them at any cost. This includes things like delivery times or warranty conditions. We piloted a new system to try to adapt to customers' requirements, like getting something very quickly or visiting people after hours. It went down extremely well. The unexpected bonus for us was that staff began to look critically at different aspects of our work and now our business has a different culture – it's able to react faster to changing circumstances and that should stand us in good stead in future in relation to some of our competitors.

Speaker 5

Trying to introduce changes in one area sometimes leads to improvements in other areas too, which you may not realize initially. We did some research recently with long-standing clients to see whether their perception of our company had altered at all. One thing that emerged was that our online renewal facility was felt by some to be less user-friendly than it might be – something we need to look into. However, a significant proportion reported that our service contracts were more tailored to their needs than in the past. After some analysis we concluded this was down to our drive to improve customer care and focus on calling clients after they'd signed up for a contract to check whether it was providing the assistance and security they wanted. An interesting outcome.

Part 3   Questions 23–30

Man: It's good to relax after all those seminars, Pam. Conferences can be intensive, can't they?

Woman: They certainly can, Mark, but they do make you think. What the last speaker said about retaining staff was interesting.

Man: Do you have problems with that?

Woman: Yes, increasingly so. We just can't keep the good people. We've been reviewing our salaries to see if that would help.

Man: Money's certainly important, at least to younger people, who've got to set up homes and all that entails. It seems less of an issue though as they go up the ladder. The perks that are part of the package, like the company car, may be more of a draw.

Woman: You may be onto something there. The last speaker implied that it was the non-material assets that kept people in place.

Man: You mean like a sunny workspace with a nice view?

Woman: Wouldn't that be nice! Didn't he mean things like, you know, a sense of being part of, not just the unit you work in, but the company as a whole. That's something you wouldn't give up lightly, though I'm not sure how you create it.

Man: I was talking to a long-standing colleague about why she'd stayed, and she said it was about knowing that what you contributed was appreciated. We have an awards scheme for high flyers, with a ceremony once a year where the MD hands out certificates. There are prizes too, like a holiday in California for the most successful salesperson. She just meant, though, getting the odd word or pat on the back from her line manager and colleagues when something had gone well.

Woman: Talking of managers, how important a role do they play?

Man: I've heard it said that people don't join a company because the managers are good, but they certainly leave because of bad ones.

Woman: That's not a cheering thought, is it, but I'm sure we've all been there. You'd think nowadays they'd be aware of the importance of assisting their staff with all these team-building courses....

Man: You'd think so, though most managers are so involved in the daily struggle to hit their targets that people just aren't an issue. Another thing – I wonder how flexible working affects staff retention.

Woman: If you mean working from home, that depends on the job. Some just don't suit that, however much you may want to do it.

Man: But there are other things, like being able to plan your core time to avoid the rush hour or collect the kids, you know. Taking six months off to explore the world sounds great too, though I think that's of limited appeal – too many financial constraints like mortgages getting in the way.

Woman: One thing we've been considering is further training.

Man: Haven't people had enough of that, what with degrees and professional qualifications?

Woman: I'm sure they have to begin with. They're delighted to spend their free time, without having to study or save up for expensive tuition. Then, later on, things get a bit samey and they're not sure where the job's leading. If a company can provide counselling and suggest what route they could take over the years, that might be the deciding factor.

Man: I think this question of the repetitiveness that comes after a few years in a post is important. Some people get to know everything about their job. They feel secure, which often suits an organisation. They're not the innovative ones though, and we need to find ways to hang onto **them**. So providing new stimuli by offering sideways moves or additional responsibilities may be one solution.

Woman: We've talked about the problems of keeping promising people, but maybe one of the hidden problems is that staff at the top aren't moving, so there's nowhere for the high flyers to go – they're stuck. Then they have to look elsewhere to get promotion.

Man: But what could you do? Move managers round on a regular basis?

Woman: Nice idea, though it might be a bit confusing for everyone. No, I was just wondering about appointing senior managers for an agreed time, say three years. That would free things up further down. It's got to be better than virtually handing good staff to our competitors, hasn't it?

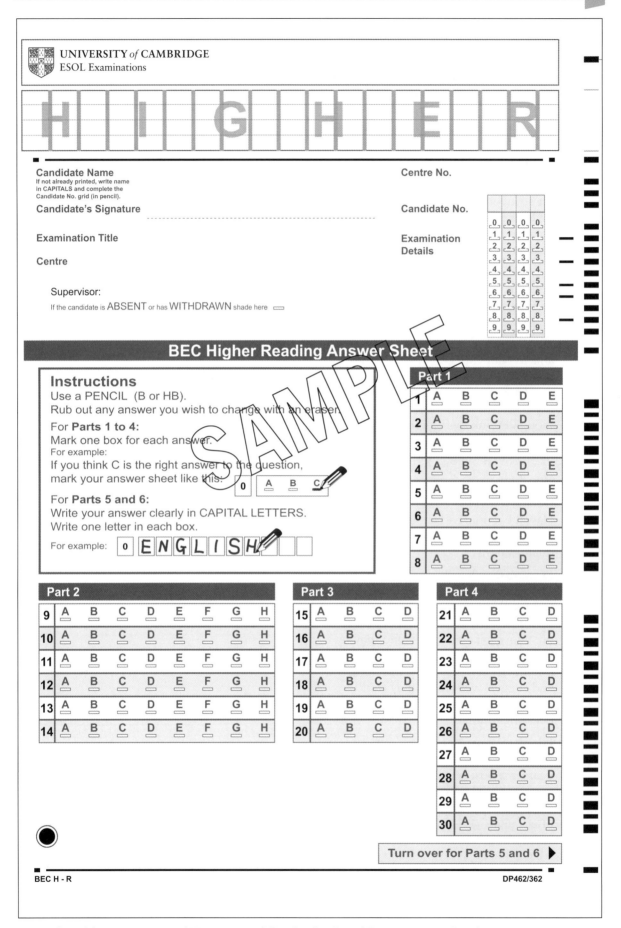

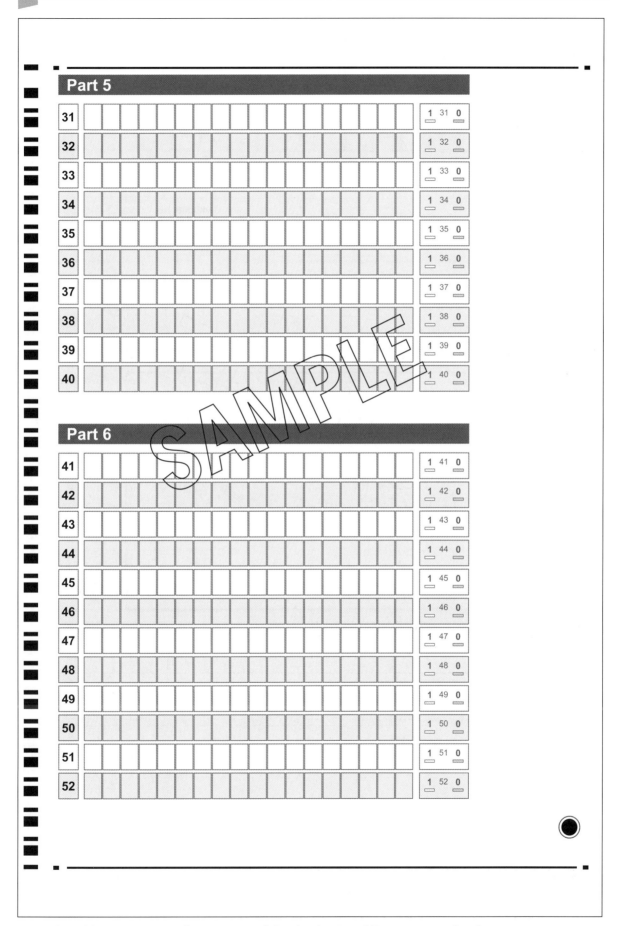

UNIVERSITY *of* **CAMBRIDGE**
ESOL Examinations

H I G H E R

Candidate Name
If not already printed, write name
in CAPITALS and complete the
Candidate No. grid (in pencil).

Candidate's Signature

Examination Title

Centre

Supervisor:
If the candidate is ABSENT or has WITHDRAWN shade here ⬜

Centre No.

Candidate No.

**Examination
Details**

BEC Higher Listening Answer Sheet

Instructions
Use a PENCIL (B or HB).
Rub out any answer you wish to change with an eraser.

For **Part 1:**
Write your answer clearly in CAPITAL LETTERS.
Write one letter or number in each box.
If the answer has more than one word, leave one box empty between words.

For example:

| 0 | Q U E S T I O N   1 2 |

For **Parts 2 and 3:**
Mark one box for each answer.

For example:
If you think C is the right answer to the question, mark your answer sheet like this:

| 0 | A | B | C |

Part 1

1   1 1 0

2   1 2 0

3   1 3 0

4   1 4 0

▶ Continue on the other side of this sheet ▶

BEC H - L   DP464/364

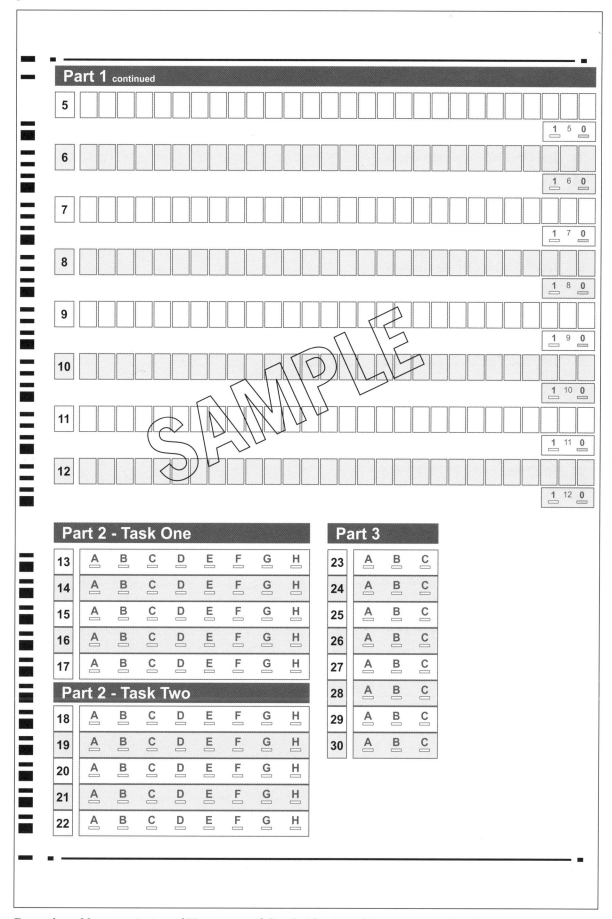

CD Track listing

Please note: Parts One, Two and Three should be played twice.

01   Test One Part One instructions
02   Test One Part One (play twice)
03   Test One Part Two instructions
04   Test One Part Two (play twice)
05   Test One Part Three instructions
06   Test One Part Three (play twice)

07   Test Two Part One instructions
08   Test Two Part One (play twice)
09   Test Two Part Two instructions
10   Test Two Part Two (play twice)
11   Test Two Part Three instructions
12   Test Two Part Three (play twice)

13   Test Three Part One instructions
14   Test Three Part One (play twice)
15   Test Three Part Two instructions
16   Test Three Part Two (play twice)
17   Test Three Part Three instructions
18   Test Three Part Three (play twice)

19   Test Four Part One instructions
20   Test Four Part One (play twice)
21   Test Four Part Two instructions
22   Test Four Part Two (play twice)
23   Test Four Part Three instructions
24   Test Four Part Three (play twice)